Beyond The Chaos

Restoring Hope for Humanity

Don Kirchner

Also by Don Kirchner

Tears of the Eagle

Return to Honor

A Matter of Time

Jewel of Saigon

Beyond The Chaos

Restoring Hope for Humanity

Don Kirchner
amatteroftime.org

Beyond The Chaos

Restoring Hope for Humanity

Don Kirchner

Special discounts and bulk quantities are available to corporations, professional associations and other organizations.
Contact us for details.
don@amatteroftime.org

No part of this book may be reproduced or transmitted in any form or by an means electronic or mechanical, including photography, recoding or by an information storage and retrieval system, without written permission from the author.

Copyright ©2023

ISBN: 978-0-578-38877-9

All Rights Reserved
Printed in the United States

Additional copies available at:
www.amatteroftime.org

Cover Photo: Don Kirchner
Book & Cover Design: Karen Reider
Editing: Cindy Davis
www.fiction-doctor.com • www.cindydavisauthor.com

To
Tom Valentine

Soul Brother, Mentor and Guide ~
A role model for
integrity, courage and the human spirit.

Foreword

By Ronald J. Thelen, M.Msc.

When Don asked me to write a Foreword for this book, my first reaction was, why me? Forewords are almost always written by someone who is a credible authority or expert in the subject matter about which a book is written, and is a way of substantiating why the author should be taken seriously.

I am a reader – an eclectic reader of some seventy-five years. In fact, I have often been called a bibliomaniac, which is a fair accusation. Over those many years I have read, studied, compared and collected thousands of volumes on many diverse subjects, so you can take this seriously. And you should.

My observation over many years is that a Foreword is often a rather personal affair between the writer of that Foreword and the author, indicating the long-standing relationship between the two. That I can do. Part of my job is to tell you about the author in a way that he does not see himself. That's going to be tough, because this author sees himself very well.

Forty years ago, I received a call from Don at my office in Los Angeles. During the ensuing conversation, it was determined that we both were owners of marketing companies and that we shared a common client who encouraged Don to call me to assist with a project he was working on. Before long, we entered into an agreement that an assistant of mine and I would commit to a four-week mutual effort to work with Don at his office to promote and market his company. The effort progressed well, and mutual respect and a strong friendship developed between us.

I returned home at the end of the fourth week and shortly thereafter, I received a call from Don's secretary. She rather crisply informed me that Don had been arrested and taken to jail on charges that were as yet unknown. A few days passed, and it was revealed that Don was a federal fugitive and was wanted on various charges having to do with drug smuggling on a rather large scale.

I had never personally known anyone charged with a federal crime, much less a fugitive from justice. To me, he had appeared to be a most forthright and honest individual, so although most perplexing, this was intriguing stuff…even somewhat exciting!

Fortunately for all of us, his experiences in federal lockup provided the basis for his first book, *A Matter Of Time,* which is now in development as a possible feature film. He went on to write his second book, *Jewel Of Saigon,* which is a novel based upon a memoir highlighting his experiences as a combat helicopter pilot in Vietnam, with a deeply romantic underlying story. All of these intense life experiences provided the basis for this book, which I believe is Don's best work to date.

I have always been a fan of parsimony, which is essentially the art of doing more with less. In the case of writing, that takes a great deal of skill and linguistic dexterity, which Don does exquisitely well…no fluff, no drawn-out, philosophical minutia. Just direct communication and application of universal truths as we have come to learn them. There are numerous references to esoteric principles, but explained specifically for the exoteric world we inhabit.

After my recent review of the first version of this book, written over a decade ago but never published, I told Don that I was so impressed with the content that I thought it was "truly inspired material." I rarely am that affected by anything I read, however in this case I am reminded of the words of Martha Graham, the visionary choreographer, about the process of inspiration. "Each of us have moments when we are swept away by an inner sense of excitement," she wrote. "In that instant, we know that something transcendent is moving within us. In some sense, it must be received."

Speaking with Don, and knowing him as I do, this is what he has expressed to me of his experience in writing this book, and this is what I have experienced in reading this finished version. During the past many years before I retired to Arizona, I was often asked to speak to various metaphysically-oriented organizations in the Los Angeles area. I can safely say that this book is a treasure trove for public speakers. Each chapter is an inspiring talk, and that's the way I hear and feel it in my mind.

Probably the most seminal encouragement found in this book was expressed by Mahatma Gandhi when he uttered his classic words, "Be the change that you want to see in the world." That's exactly what Don has done, and in so doing he has unveiled a mystery. By changing yourself, you can ultimately affect the world in a positive way.

Finally, a word of advice to you, the reader: When you purchase or receive this book, first read it from cover to cover. Then, in your wisdom, should you decide to proceed further, read each chapter again, 1 to 12, but one at a time. Reflect on the information, take a few notes and begin to practice what you have noted. You will begin to experience a change in your life, hopefully for the better. When this begins to occur, others will be affected by your change, and for you an entirely new perspective and outlook on life may develop, or continue if you've already begun. I also highly recommend that you read the Introduction.

Ronald J. Thelen, M.Msc.
Chino Valley, AZ
October 7, 2021

Introduction

When I wrote the first version of this book, *Return to Honor,* over a dozen years ago, America was in deep trouble. It was 2008, and the real estate bubble had burst so dramatically that real estate lost its historical status as the most secure collateral to own. For the first time in eight decades, America's economy was collapsing and another Depression seemed imminent. The value of homes in my community and across the nation spiraled out of control so fast that we couldn't catch up, resulting in a foreclosure sale of our home and the loss of blood, sweat, tears and hard-earned money invested in it. Our safe little haven was gone in less time than it took to drive back from Washington State where we were developing a book publishing and film production business. With little tangible means of income, we were forced to reinvent ourselves at a time when nothing felt safe anymore, and the concept of "normal" had vanished.

Sound familiar?

Now it's 2021, and things are far worse…even with the worst apparently over and the economy on some sort of upswing. However, there's strong evidence of another surge of COVID-19 coming on strong, politics are the most divisive and dysfunctional in our entire history, and climate change appears to be accelerating beyond the predictions of even the most alarmist of climate scientists. It's not a good time for die-hard optimists like myself.

But in several ways not yet entirely clear to me, it could prove to be one of the best years for me in the past couple of decades because I have refused to buy into a doomsday scenario or government conspiracy theories. Any of that could ultimately prove to be real, however I've seen and feared many such scenarios in my time on Earth and I'm still here, still in relatively good health, and things are looking up. In writing that, I offer my deepest and most heartfelt respects and condolences to the families and friends of the many souls who departed this past year because of all things COVID-related, and to people who have suffered the loss of homes, jobs, and other misfortunes that have happened to them during this time. It has been for all of them, and for people around the globe, a very challenging time from which there seems little hope for anything good to come from it.

That said and acknowledged, I will nevertheless encourage you to stay open to the prospects of hope and better times ahead. What I will present in the following chapters may prove to be more than mere hope. In fact, having endured the ravages of the "Great Recession" of 2008, and now the pandemic and near breakdowns in politics, the economy and climate change, I can tell you without hesitation that there is promise of a decent future for us yet. But only if we can embrace the premise that with every challenge comes opportunity for growth, learning and advancement. To the extent that you are willing to suspend your doubts and fears long enough to read and reflect on what I am presenting in these chapters, you as an individual may find yourself keenly aware of principles and insights that are available to you that can bring you deep relief that all is not so bad as it may seem. You might find some of your most important perspectives on life changing to the extent that all may not be as dismal as it appears to be.

Throughout our history, there is ample evidence of good things having evolved from very dark times because humanity saw fit to collectively learn from each experience…be it tyrannical leaders, wars or calamities. The "Golden Age" of the Renaissance came about at the end of the worst of times in our history – the Dark Ages – which lasted *four hundred years*. The good news about that is it's not going to take us four hundred years to get through this…or even forty. Provided we can make it through all the deception, misguided thinking, and emotional imbalances of present times, we have the Internet, social media, modern technology, and newer generations of brilliant young souls that all together can get humanity through it in less time than that. But only if we put our collective hearts and minds into to finding and fully embracing innovative solutions.

It will take a lot of cooperation and collaboration, tolerance and patience. That's essentially what this book is about, but it has to start with you, the individual – more now than ever before in our history. I have learned that you can't do much of anything really meaningful for or with anyone else if you don't first consider the person in the mirror and what matters the most – true integrity, authenticity, and personal honor.

It is the purpose of this book to simply present those principles and insights as evidence of things and events in my past, and now present, that have enabled me to see beyond what appears in the dark, black clouds of fear storms of the greatest magnitude I have seen in my lifetime, to catch a glimpse of the bluest skies and brightest sunlight I could have imagined going into either of these very difficult periods.

There is something sensible and practical in these chapters that is drawn from ancient teachings and wisdom of the Ages that might help you better understand why things are the way they are, and how you as an individual can take meaningful steps to make them better – for yourself and for many others with whom you might feel moved to share your experience.

You may be pleasantly surprised. I have been, many times over. Both the "Great Recession" and now COVID-19 have been good for me, but only because I was able to "step back" in my mind and see the bigger picture. I lost my home, business and people dearest to me in the former, and suffered through along with everyone else during the ravages of the latter, but I gained far more from each of them than I lost. As you will read, each of these chapters shows how and why the same can happen for you.

I look forward to getting through the coming challenges that I believe are ahead of us, and to the new "Renaissance" that I believe we can create from the upheavals we are all living through…and many are dying from. There is a reason for it to be the way it is, and I think it could well be to get us to what we all need and want…peace of mind, respect for each other and sensible lives and futures not just for our children and their children, but for us as well in our lifetimes.

As a modern-day sage declared only a few years ago to a group of forward thinkers gathered to contemplate the tumultuous times ahead, he said with index finger pointed upward, "In all of human history, this is *the* time to be alive."

I say, "Bring it on…"

Don Kirchner
Sedona, AZ
July 21, 2021

Contents

Foreword by Ronald J. Thelen, M.Msc. vi

Introduction by Don Kirchner ix

1   Honor 1

2   Purpose 13

3   Passion 27

4   Courage 43

5   Attitude 57

6   Truth 69

7   Trust 79

8   Integrity 93

9   The Injunctions 107

10   Compassion 121

11   Detachment 131

12   The Human Spirit .143

     Resources 161

     About the Author .167

"No person was ever honored for what he received. Honor has been the reward for what he gave."

– Calvin Coolidge

CHAPTER ONE

Honor

It is my prime objective with this book to do whatever I can to bring respect, sanity and balance into the world by any means possible. I have a message and a voice and, like Martin Luther King, I too have a dream. That dream is to see the day when people of all colors, cultures, and backgrounds treat one another with respect, and live their lives with the sense of dignity and caring that characterized older generations of bygone eras when people lived and died by the good reputations they had built. To them, truth, respect, and honor were not merely words but a way of life. A person's word was their bond, and agreements were often sealed with only a handshake.

Perhaps those are only myths and stereotyped roles in movies and television dramas, but I believe it's really the way things can be, and should be. I believe it's not only possible to restore a sense of that nobility and decency to our society; it's even probable…*if* we want that enough. I believe in the power of collective consciousness, which is to say that if enough of us started believing it's possible, and acted as if it's already happening, we will soon see a measurable shift in the way things are today.

Who hasn't felt uplifted and inspired by movies like *Pay It*

Forward, Remember The Titans or *Gladiator*? I realize there are certain realities of life we cannot escape or ignore, such as gravity, earth, fire and oxygen, however there are other more subtle realities portrayed in movies and stories that are just as real, and they bring about changes whether we notice them or not. One of those realities is that when enough people think differently, and then act accordingly, others change by mere exposure at a level and a rate that can become dramatic and even miraculous.

Years ago, there was a bumper sticker campaign called "Random Acts of Kindness." For a while, it became popular enough that people changed their attitudes towards each other in noticeable ways such that it appeared as if it might take off. The movie *Pay It Forward*, which was about the power of kindness and the ripple effects that can result in attitude changes on a massive scale, illustrated that power in a most dramatic way. For a while, it was amazing to experience. On the Golden Gate Bridge, people started paying the toll fees for five or ten cars behind them. Once the nightly newscasters began reporting daily totals, it turned into a competition of sorts with unknown drivers attempting to outdo each other.

People in grocery store checkout lines suddenly had their groceries paid for by shoppers who had checked out before them. Baristas in coffee shops reported an upsurge in customers adding $5 or $10 to their bill to pass on to the next few customers. I even had that happen to me recently at a Starbucks drive-through window, and it had me feeling great all day long…especially since that fad seemed to have faded out years ago.

Change comes when enough people transform their thinking

long enough for it to take effect on others. It may not come packaged the way we expect or want it to come, or it may come in such a subtle way that we don't notice it at first...*but it will come.* History bears this out over and over again. The greatest changes come not from large movements, as noted by a famous anthropologist, but rather in small groups with passion enough to bring about change because the cause is right and appropriate to the common need. I'm such a believer in the strength and power of kindness to change things I will issue a challenge to anyone who will make an effort to show kindness to others in some meaningful way.

If it turns out this book was the cause of the inspiration, I will match whatever that action was...within reason, of course. Perhaps that will give you added incentive if you're thinking you might start something, but keep in mind it works best if it's anonymous. It's okay to do good things and receive recognition for it, but it's so much more effective when it happens without people's egos and emotions getting caught up in it. I'll add my contact information at the end of the book along with listings of resources, people and organizations you can join or at least be aware of, and become part of something organized. Until then, experiment with small things and do it often enough and consistently enough that you will notice changes in attitudes of others around you, even with just a pleasant attitude, a smile or a kind act. You'll be amazed if you pay attention...anonymously.

Speaking of small groups making the biggest changes in collective consciousness, consider Martin Luther King and the civil rights movement. It began with people like Rosa Parks not giving up her seat to a white man on a bus in Montgomery, Alabama in 1955, and grew to sit-ins at luncheon counters and small protests by black people who risked their lives doing so. Look at how different things are now since that movement began. There is still racial prejudice, but it doesn't have nearly the power it once did because enough people of all races realized how bad it really was and how much it needed to change. People think differently about race now, and even though many people still have some of the same motivations their predecessors did, at least they're now more challenged and not as able to get away with it so flagrantly as back then. Eventually, new generations will never have heard the term "colored" in reference to another person or race.

Change is coming, like it or not. When things get so off-balance that airliners are skyjacked and flown into skyscrapers, and we can't build prisons fast enough or large enough to accommodate what has become the #1 per capita rate of incarceration in the world, something has to give. When 75% of people interviewed nationwide say that they hate their jobs and are unhappy with their lives, something's very wrong with the Land of the Free and the Home of the Brave. This is increasingly evidenced in newspaper headlines and daily news. Random shootings have become so commonplace that even the most brutal among them have become just so much tabloid fodder.

I want to be part of change that's positive and beneficial rather than be subjected to the insanity of drive-by shootings, road rage, and the political divisiveness and bitterness we live with today. I'm not talking about creating some kind of utopia or survivalist, garrison mentality, but a truly egalitarian society where people respect each other as human beings first and foremost, and have equal rights and opportunities that aren't just noble words on parchment paper, or legislative acts that get lost in political priorities. There is only one way I know how to accomplish that, and that's getting as many people as possible to think respectfully, and act that way toward each other *without further delay*. Respect for each other and for common human decency should be sacrosanct, and our top priority.

That kind of change in individual thinking and behaving can and will alter collective attitudes and reasoning that can bring desperately needed changes while still allowing for other people's beliefs, doctrines, and philosophies to be upheld, valued, and respected, the way we started out as a nation. It will even allow for those who have committed crimes to be punished, yet to also be treated with a modicum of respect so that there will be a bridge back, with better incentive for them to change their behavior by our example. Over two and a half million people – men, women, and children – are locked up on any given day in this country, and over eleven million have done time or are in some sort of criminal justice supervision. That seems to bear out the premise that harsh punishment isn't working.

> *Respect for each other and for common decency should be sacrosanct, and our top priority.*

Why not? Because there is no respect on either side. Social psychologists will bear me out on this…that lack of common decency and respect between people leads to apathy, resentment and avarice. To respect someone does not necessarily mean to agree with them or condone their way of thinking or living. It just means their lives matter, and they have a right to at least be heard and valued. It's one of the fundamental needs that all human beings have, to be heard and to be valued as something more than just another warm body among billions of others.

The purpose of this book is to share with you some insights gained in my first half-century-plus on this planet, during which we as a nation have experienced some pretty dramatic changes in people's thinking, one of which was the civil rights movement. I have met and worked with teachers, forward thinkers and philosophers who have influenced cultural and behavioral changes on a grand scale. They also believe we can make a meaningful difference in the way things are by a large-scale shift in thinking and acting by humanity. For most of the last century, apartheid in South Africa was so powerful it was thought nothing could change it, and yet by the end of the century, a small movement had grown to the point where its leader, Nelson Mandela, became the first democratically elected black President of South Africa…after spending over twenty years in prison.

Change does happen, and now with high-tech communications and social media to connect us on a global scale with each other faster and more effectively, it happens faster and more frequently, with astonishing results – politically, economically and socially – even spiritually. But there is something at the core of all of the changing and need for changing that is more important than changing simply for the sake of changing. That's human evolution, which mystics and prognosticators and forward thinkers all agree, is something we are all involved with perhaps more so than at any other time in human history.

Honor is synonymous with respect. Respecting others, respecting

Self, respecting life and the rights of others to exist. It needs no explanation or justification. It is fundamental to any civilized society to respect life in all its forms. Without it, we are little more than primitive beings no matter how advanced we might be with technology, medicine, education, or government. Respect is the ability and willingness to see and at least allow for another persons point of view without judging, qualifying, or demeaning them, regardless of their background, culture, or personal history. By respect, I don't mean agreeing with or tolerating inappropriate or bad behavior, but rather being willing to allow each other a fundamental measure of decency and the dignity of being alive and of value. To me, that's what honor is all about…respecting people for who they are and what they believe. You can do that as a Christian, Jew, Muslim or Hindu, Catholic or atheist. You can also do it as a prison guard, a warden, or as an inmate.

> Respect is the ability and willingness to see and at least allow for another persons point of view without judging, qualifying, or demeaning them.

That's the attitude upon which the foundation of this country was built, and enabled it to grow strong until recent decades during which it has become in the minds of many people in other countries an attitude of "bullying" that disrespects others' laws, customs and heritage. The kindness and generosity we showed the world after WWII has mutated over the decades into such a mish-mash of laws and vague notions of morality and an image to the world that "might makes right," so no one seems to know what is right anymore. It has become a form of arrogance, and a disrespect of a global, nationalized kind, and a product of our own collective disrespect for ourselves and for what our past generations stood for and believed in.

I believe we can change the system and make this a better place to live and to bring more joy and fulfillment into our lives. These are fundamental elements of restoring a sense of honor to our society by starting with the individual. They may or may not be fundamental to you, but ultimately they need to be because without them there is only indifference and disrespect at all levels that can and does run rampant.

What makes me such an expert on this subject? One of those "miracles" I referred to earlier was surviving the U.S. prison system where I managed to turn what was likely to become a twenty-five-year sentence without chance of parole into two-and-a-half years of actual time served, and earning the respect of my presiding judge, my prosecutor, correctional officials, and even inmates I encountered along the way. The only way through that experience as an educated, white, middle-aged male with any chance of a positive outcome was to find the courage and respect within myself and bring it out in others around me in a place where honor and respect are very different things to different people.

Out of sheer survival, I quickly discovered there were some common moral values behind the angry, scarred, and tattooed faces and gladiator types that had to do with respect and human dignity at the most basic level of survival. You can't fake that kind of respect. It has to be real and genuine, or you'll be eaten alive. I was moved around a lot, so I was forced by circumstances to get it down quickly and make it real. I had to genuinely care about others and their circumstances before I could expect them to care about me or my needs and wants. Once I understood it, it served me so well that a very bleak-looking future turned around, and prison for me turned out to be more like a tour of duty and one of the most profound learning experiences of my life.

That carried me through those years and the years afterward in business and academics, then later on back into prisons and jails as a respected teacher, mentor, and criminal justice advocate. I went back as a man with a message of genuine hope and real promise of freedom for those who wanted to change and improve their lives by cultivating compassion in helping others improve theirs.

Embraced powerfully by enough people, change for the better *will* come…slowly at first, then faster as more people experience the truth and the power of compassion and caring. Within our lifetimes, we can experience a point of "critical mass," where indifference and lack of caring will be a thing of the past, just like segregation and apartheid is now. From there, we can build it in many different and amazing ways until we discover what Martin Luther King was really dreaming about.

It was, and still is, *freedom*…of the human spirit. I want that point of critical mass to come sooner than later, so I'm writing this book to do my part to make that come to pass *now*, while I'm still able to enjoy it. Wouldn't that be something for the media to report, and talk show hosts to cover? Random Acts of Kindness becoming a way of life and not just a bumper sticker? "Pay It Forward" as a defining characteristic of our nation and even other nations, rather than just a feel-good movie? A "kinder, gentler nation" that really means something instead of being just an empty political campaign slogan?

We owe it to our children and grandchildren to leave something behind that has more substance than just material things. We must instill in them a high moral value they can feel and understand and be proud of as they build their lives and futures. If we are willing to embrace just a few of the core values and principles I discovered while hacking and slashing my way through a jungle of self-deception and misguided loyalties while a paved highway was within easy reach, we as a society can stop the mindless waging of war on everything perceived as a threat or offensive to us. We can then begin to enjoy our children and the fruits of all our efforts in a vastly improved world *now,* while we're still alive.

In order to do that, we have to begin with ourselves, to learn how it takes root inside of us and how it spreads. It's a matter of perception and pre-conceived notions, which we can stop as easily as turning off a faucet. But it takes practice and vigilance because keeping that faucet turned on has become such a pervasive habit, reinforced over and over again by the media and by reactive, fear-based thinking over which we believe we have no control. It may take a while to see and feel the benefits of changing our thinking, but it can happen in relatively short order once enough people begin to embrace the notion and make it a way of life.

One of the first things we will experience will be less stress and more peace of mind. Then comes a collective sense of purpose, passion, and value. With that, we will believe we all have value, and that we matter to others – not just to friends and family, but to the grocery store clerk, the banker, and even government bureaucrats we may never meet. If people know they matter to you, then they will embrace the notion, even if only subconsciously, that you do, too. You don't have to accept or condone aberrant behavior of people, but you can respect their existence on the planet. Your life will improve a little bit at a time, or a lot, depending on how well and how soon you catch on and pass it on to others.

If enough people do that, we will reduce crime, change attitudes of gang members, and reduce school and random shootings. We'll see sanity and balance return to our world and, what's more, we can do it soon enough to be able to take full credit for it as a generation that ushered in the "New Renaissance."

It can happen in our lifetimes.

*"There is no greater gift
you can give or receive
than to honor your calling.
It's why you were born.
And how you become most truly alive."*

– Oprah Winfrey

CHAPTER TWO
Purpose

There are few questions more perplexing than, "What is my purpose?' In all of the turmoil of our present-day world, and especially after living through the ravages of 2020, that question has even more significance now. On the surface, we may feel there are more practical matters to attend to, like mortgages, education, raising our children, etc. But there are few things over our lifetimes that perplex us more than wondering what we're doing here, and what our purpose is in Life. As someone who has come into close contact with people of many walks of life, I have found this to be universally true. Hospice workers will confirm this is the most common lament among their patients as they draw closer to their passing – that they never identified or achieved their true life's purpose.

In his classic memoir, *Man's Search for Meaning,* psychiatrist Viktor Frankl wrote of his three-and-a-half years in Nazi concentration camps and the life-and-death struggles he and his fellow prisoners endured every day. He discovered almost without exception that anyone who managed to maintain a sense of purpose and meaning, even under those horrific conditions, seemed to be in the right place at the right time. "They always had a light in their eyes," Dr. Frankl wrote, "no matter how emaciated they became." He went on to write about how those who lost their sense of purpose and value were either dead or gone within days, if not hours. "Their eyes would actually turn grey and lifeless," he recalled, "and it happened so frequently it became predictable."

That book had a powerful impact on me. I received it from a man in federal prison who was serving four concurrent life sentences for murder. His name was Jim Valentine, but he was known by everyone only as "Big Jim." It wasn't because he was physically that big, but because he had a big presence just the way he carried himself. He *felt* big. His first offense had been an accident when he was barely eighteen, but it involved an off-duty cop who was bullying a younger friend of his. They got into a tussle and when they both fell back against a stone wall, the man's head hit the wall first and the blow killed him. Someone noticed his badge, and Jim panicked. A scared young kid, he ran away confused and terrified. Now labeled a "cop-killer," he didn't stand much of a chance of surviving the manhunt that ensued. In the frenzy to capture him in the rugged mountains where he had grown up, another cop was killed in the hail of bullets, and everything went downhill from there. He was captured and spent several years in prison in Colorado until he managed to escape. The next one came months later when he was caught in Ohio, but not before another cop was killed by his own fellow officers, according to Jim, but he was blamed for it and received another life sentence. The fourth was a guard who was tormenting a young inmate who had done nothing wrong, and made the mistake of turning his back on Big Jim. None of the murders was premeditated, so the sentences were concurrent rather than consecutive, which gave him a chance for parole after twenty years.

At one point during those twenty years of unimaginably brutal conditions, Jim read Viktor Frankl's book and realized that his personal journey wasn't about guilt or innocence, but about personal freedom of a different kind – one that not many people can imagine would come out the way it did for him. The book probably saved my life too, by enabling me to discover the power of the human spirit to overcome adversity. I had very little experience with incarceration, and Jim could see it right away. Once we began talking respectfully with each other, he made a point on occasion of openly standing by me in the cellblock, thereby indicating to everyone we were friends. When he was transferred a few days later, he left the book for me. It changed my entire outlook on life, and to this day right choice of attitude remains my primary guiding principle.

Big Jim discovered that he could write, which turned into a number of articles he published about prison life for magazines. A major magazine eventually gave him his own column on life in prison. When I first met him, he was about to be paroled and had a job lined up with the magazine as an Associate Editor, *after twenty years' imprisonment.* By following his new-found passion for writing, a path toward a whole new future emerged that he could not have previously imagined. He had found his purpose and his value in life, and that set him free in a much more meaningful way than simply being released from confinement.

I was at the beginning of my prison journey when I met him. He knew that with no prior experience in confinement and no means of protecting myself from what lay ahead, I was headed for trouble. His words to me in the brief time I had with him made the difference between certain hell and a powerful learning experience that ultimately led me to my own freedom. "Find something to be grateful for every day that you get up," he said. "No matter how difficult things get, they will get better for you."

I always thought I had a pretty good sense of my purpose, but suddenly I was in prison without a clue as to how I managed to get there under such bizarre circumstances. I couldn't imagine at the time how things might get any better for me without a miracle. Because of the nature of the people I had been involved with, and the size of their operation, I was looking at some pretty serious time to figure it all out.

> *Find something to be grateful for every day that you get up, and no matter how difficult things get, they will get better for you.*

But it didn't take long once I saw a way to turn things around despite it looking pretty hopeless. As a thirty-five-year old, white, educated male, I stood out among inmates and officers as someone different from them, and certainly not to be trusted by any of them on either side.

Within a few months, however, I discovered I could do something useful. I had a good education and I spoke rudimentary Spanish, so I was able to assist the few inmates who would talk with me who couldn't read or write to send letters to their families. To some extent, I was able to help some of them understand their legal documents. Gradually, I developed some trust among the Hispanics until I was able to obtain GED materials and taught them basic reading and writing until I had "classes" that attracted the attention of officers and staff at the various facilities where I was housed during my time in the system.

Little did I realize at the time that these first actions were the underpinnings of a different purpose for my life, and what would become a new path for me. At first, tutoring was an act of survival on my part. If I could assist others with things that mattered to them, I might be less likely to be suspected as a possible informant. As the months passed and I was moved several times, I began to sense an entirely different motive and purpose growing in me. To see and experience changes in behavior and attitudes of men filled with anger, hatred and bitterness into men willing to respect each other – even with officers and staff – was immensely rewarding for me. It formed the basis of an entirely new outlook on what the journey was really about for me.

Inmate's and officer's attitudes toward me changed noticeably, even with successive moves from one place to another, and gradually positive write-ups appeared in my records. Letters of commendation from high-ranking supervisors followed me back to federal court where I faced multiple charges for crimes I didn't commit. Because I was guilty by association (conspiracy), and couldn't prove I hadn't taken part in all of their criminal activities, I could have been found guilty of everything I was charged with.

Meanwhile, as he was preparing for hearings and my eventual trial, the prosecutor in the case read the write-ups and commendation letters in my files, which did not fit the picture he had in his mind about me. In an unprecedented move after a critical pre-trial hearing, he had me brought to his office late in the evening for an unofficial, off-the-record meeting. Suddenly, when everything was looking hopeless for me, I had a rare opportunity to tell my side of the story to

Purpose

the "enemy" – the one person who could possibly make a difference in my case – without having to testify against anyone.

I had found my purpose. It was becoming clear in my growing official legal record that I was making a positive difference in the attitudes and behavior of other inmates, *and* with correctional officers who observed and even participated to some extent. My inspiration came from men who wanted to change their lives but had no apparent means of accomplishing that. The letters and comments in my files, together with my attitude in the courtroom, were enough to cause the prosecutor to rethink his position and take steps to change the outcome. Of his own volition, he dropped two of the most serious charges, including the racketeering provision which would have denied any chance of parole. Most importantly, as he wrote in his Foreword to my first book, he went out on a limb to help me because he was moved by a growing sense of respect and some degree of compassion.

> *Inspiration comes in many different forms, but I believe it's inextricably linked to a sense of purpose.*

Inspiration comes in many different forms, but I believe it's inextricably linked to a sense of purpose. You can feel when someone is aligned with their purpose in life, and when they are not. Who doesn't feel good when they hear of someone who pushes through obstacles and achieves success through determination? Who isn't inspired by stories of Mother Theresa, Martin Luther King, Abraham Lincoln, or Gandhi? Each of them developed a sense of purpose, and they did so by letting go of beliefs they had about what they should do and instead did what they felt called to do by an inner drive to do the right thing. They devoted themselves to their *soul's calling,* and they moved mountains.

Gandhi, for example, was a lawyer when he traveled to South Africa on business. There he encountered intense racial hatred and drew the wrath of the white Afrikaans who were in power. He witnessed and suffered through discrimination at its worst, and he changed his course and his entire purpose in life as a result. His acts of courage eventually brought the British Empire's colonial rule over India to an end, which ultimately led to the end of apartheid in South Africa many years later. He also quelled virtual genocide over religious differences between Muslims and Hindus without ever using guns or violence to bring this about.

Mother Theresa had a desire to teach, and to serve God, so she became a Roman Catholic nun and missionary and devoted her life to teaching and easing human suffering. That was purposeful and noble, but as I later learned from reading about her life, it wasn't really her soul's calling. She felt specifically drawn to the sick and dying, but was unable to receive permission to dedicate herself to that work. She eventually became so moved by her sense of purpose that she left the convent to follow her calling. In time, she developed such a widespread following that the Pope personally called on her and allowed her to start her own order. She created the Missionaries of Charity in 1950, and by 2012 the organization had 4,500 nuns and was active in 133 countries.

Both these individuals began as simple people. Abraham Lincoln was another one. In his early years, he was a mundane politician who actually failed in repeated attempts to secure even low-level political office. But he was a gifted orator, and a man with a sense of purpose.

Undaunted by failures, he learned from them and increased his sense of purpose enough to eventually run for President of the United States, *and won*. His sense of purpose gave him drive and direction, fueled his passion and inspired him to go way beyond his perceived limitations. Repeated "failure" did not deter him from his course, and he went on to end slavery and become one of the most beloved of all American Presidents.

Like compassion, inspiration is infectious. It compels people to do things they would not ordinarily do – even those who are merely observers. People can be motivated to do things differently, but inspired people do extraordinary things – things they would never have imagined they could do. Lance Armstrong, prior to his Tour d'France victories, was bedridden with cancer when his wife brought a new racing bicycle to his hospital room and left it by his bed. That inspired him to get out of bed and begin exercising that gradually enabled him to get outside and put it, and himself, to better use. While we may not be legendary athletes like Lance Armstrong,[1] neither was he at that point in his life.

Inspired people do great things because they discovered there is a purpose for their lives and a reason for their existence beyond personal gain. Ironically, finding your own purpose and using it to improve the lives of others often attracts additional unexpected income, credibility, social acceptance and personal power. Living one's true purpose is personal power because it comes from one's *soul*...one's very Being.

---

[1] Ed. Note: Lance Armstrong later admitted to using performance-enhancing drugs and was stripped of all titles, however that does not alter the point or significance of finding one's purpose.

One of my favorite stories of heroism is Medal of Honor recipient Audie Murphy. Audie was the most highly decorated soldier in US military history. In WWII, he single-handedly held off six enemy tanks and waves of German soldiers with one machine gun, despite being seriously wounded. This enabled his men to fortify and secure their positions until reinforcements came and drove the Germans back. Besides the Medal of Honor, he earned a total of 33 medals and awards for bravery.

The thing that speaks to me most about his story is a humble quote about what drove him to such extremes in battle. When asked what enabled him to accomplish such feats of courage, he said, "Once I got over my initial cowardice, I realized that it's what I went there to do. It was my purpose for being there."

History books, movies, and novels are filled with stories like this – of heroes and leaders who emerged from the common masses and did incredible things. Often we learn later that these visionaries never had any prior notions of greatness or daring. In some way or another, they each found their purpose and used it to follow a new path. This can happen to anyone at any time if they're willing to listen to their inner guidance. Beyond spiritual connotations and principles, this inner guidance represents the soul calling out. We all have a soul, and it has a voice. It's encoded with our purpose, and it's what we came here to do or to become in our time on Earth. Regardless of any of our physical, cultural, or economic attributes, we all have it in us to find our purpose. For some, it may be to pull a rickshaw through the streets of New Delhi, or grow orchids in England. Whatever it is for you, it's vital to your true success in life to find it, align with it and trust it to take you where you need to go. It doesn't have to be glorious victories on battlefields, or bringing down tyrannies. It can be as simple as growing gardens, painting canvases, or writing books. To find it takes a willingness to cultivate and follow your own intuition.

Intuition, for most of us, is a virtue that's rarely cultivated and seldom followed. It's the sort of thing that is often frowned upon or thought of as frivolous or "New Agey." But the power contained in one's intuition is a power that can move mountains…or armies. For anyone with an interest in or fascination with the game of chess, there is an interesting interpretation of the meaning and purpose of the game and its pieces, which has much to do with intuition. According to Manley P. Hall, one of the more evolved philosophers of the mid-twentieth century, each part of it represents some aspect of the human psyche. The board represents life, and the two colors represent its dark and light polarities. The King represents the Soul, which can never be removed from the board (life). The Queen, the most powerful piece on the board, represents the mind. It can move in any direction and can capture any opponent's piece.

Ironically, the lowly pawns (of which there are eight), can capture a queen if it's in a vulnerable position. The pawn represents the intuition, and each pawn has the power to become any piece its player wants it to be if it reaches the opponent's back rank. According to this rule of the game, it could be said that theoretically, intuition has eight times the power of the mind.

"Chess is hardly a game," wrote Hall. "It's an exercise for the human psyche. It was invented by God's angels to give humanity a way to keep themselves free from mental and spiritual manipulation, and egos under control." To draw on chess as a metaphor, every time

I've brought my queen out too early in the game (of life), I've lost her. Only when circumstances forced me to slow down and rely more on my intuition, and creativity (the knights), did I begin to feel my way through the messes I created with all of my cleverness and ego, and learn to use my mind in a more intelligent, balanced way.

When one allows for balance between the more subtle aspects of the mind, things take shape in ways that some people might call "miraculous." This happened for me with increasing frequency to the point where I no longer thought of them as coincidences or miracles.

> *When one allows for balance between the more subtle aspects of the mind, things take shape in ways that some people might call "miraculous."*

One of the most dramatic miracles was my prosecutor who altered the outcome of my case in a way that was unprecedented and astonishing.

Physically and emotionally, those were very challenging years for me, but they turned out to be the most rewarding times of my life. I learned more about myself and my purpose than I might ever have discovered otherwise. For most of my first year in prison, I used my ability to win over inmates so I could prove to authorities that I belonged on the outside. I was doing good things with my ability, but for the wrong reasons. My case just kept getting worse, no matter how well I appeared to be doing. Then, just as it got to the point where it couldn't seem to go downhill any further, I had a revelation.

As I mentioned previously, I was moved through the federal prison system quite a bit. When prisoners are moved through the system, they are generally kept in solitary confinement simply because the staff and officers don't know their background. One of

Purpose   Beyond The Chaos

my moves came during a particularly hard time for me, combined with an equipment breakdown that kept me on "holdover" status at one particularly dismal facility longer than I should have been there. What ensued for me was a four-day long, soul-wrenching experience in solitary confinement in a dark and dingy cell that became for me a life-or-death ordeal. I imagined a dragon alone with me in that cell. I couldn't eat or sleep the entire time I was there. Finally, I was forced by sheer mental and emotional exhaustion, to give up what had become a raging mental battle with the image of this fire-breathing beast intent on devouring me. I began to hear a voice inside – a voice the likes of which I'd never heard before.

    Clearly, I knew it was inside my head, but it had a certain tone and meaning to it. It was a wise, older voice that had a sense of calmness and knowing. An inner dialog ensued in my head which I was able to transcribe word for word on paper I had nearby. Although completely internal, it was the most sensible, profound dialog I'd ever heard. It was so clear and sharp I had no doubt I was in touch with some deeply intelligent, wise part of myself. There was no judgment, criticism, or blame associated with any of the comments, and at one point, it became so comfortable that it was actually a bit humorous. And then it was gone.

    From that point on, a different version of "me" was in charge. I felt there was a paternal, or perhaps ancestral presence, watching over me. Gradually at first, but then more frequently as the days and weeks passed, I found myself slowing down and hesitating before I said or did anything. It was as if a close friend was with me, and watching through my eyes everything I did, said, or thought. Attitudes of those with whom I came in contact seemed more open and receptive, and I was treated differently than before. I felt a distinctly different personality taking shape, and my thinking became more measured and reflective. That change continues to this day, and motivates me to get up each morning with a sense of gratitude for a purpose that I had not experienced before.

What's *your* purpose? Do you have a desire and the willingness to make a commitment to trust yourself, to trust your own inner voice no matter what? If you do, you're on the right track.

"God Promised us a Safe Harbor," I read on a large poster once, depicting a kayaker paddling furiously through wild rapids smashing through towering rock formations and cliffs way above his head. At the bottom was, "But not necessarily a safe passage." I smile every time I think of that poster. It has come to mind so many times since then as I have paddled through rapids of my own making…even a Niagara Falls at one point that could have been the end of me.

Occasionally, I remembered some of these stories enough to let go and trust in my sense of purpose. Every time I did, something good happened, even if it didn't show up right away. More than a few times, virtual miracles took place. I think it's safe to say I'm trusting it now.

If you want your life to change, you will have to change with it. It won't work until you do. It might seem like you are, but you may have to work on yourself for a while until you are forced by circumstances or by some awakening to align yourself with your true purpose.

When you do, you'll be ready for miracles.

"A true passion that burns within your soul is one that can never be put out."

– Zach Toelke

CHAPTER THREE

Passion

Passion is a term so commonly used that most everyone thinks they know what it is. But like the terms Love, Honor and Truth, there are so many different usages and meanings of the terms that it's difficult to accurately describe or define them. Some people are very passionate about some things, while others aren't at all…about anything.

To me, passion is a fire inside of you that fuels you – or not – to get up each day and make your way in the world. It's what keeps you going besides the need to pay the rent or the mortgage. You may only have a little bit of passion to stay alive and keep holding on, or you may have a lot of it that keeps you awake at night with a longing to do something bigger, bolder and better. Passion is like electricity. It's available for all to use, but how we use it and to what degree, is very different from the average person just getting by, to someone who uses its full power to drive them to levels of personal accomplishment beyond most people's imaginations.

To use another metaphor, as a pilot I can say that passion is to our lives like the throttle of an airplane. At partial power, you can take off and, if the winds are right and there are no adverse conditions, you might make it to your destination. Getting there, however, can be

Passion

tricky…fraught with hazards and unexpected challenges that may prevent you from arriving safely. Passion is the necessary ingredient to fuel a dream or desire, and enables you to achieve your full potential in life. Passion makes everything work. Without it, or with just some passion, you can get by and you can even appear to be successful. But you won't enjoy the journey nearly as much, nor will you be likely to achieve your full potential in life. Passion turns the mundane into the extraordinary.

The musical, *Chicago,* comes to mind as an example of passion at work on the stage and in the theatre. I was enchanted and even entranced with every song, dance, and set design. Every time I watch any of the Golden Buzzer performances on *America's Got Talent* and *Britain's Got Talent*, it brings tears to my eyes, especially when the winner is a young child or disabled person. What drives them to achieve those hights is pure passion and desire. There are many good examples, but one in particular that comes strongly to mind because it involves more than sheer talent is Mandy Harvey. Mandy had great talent, but she encountered a debilitating obstacle. She was a singer from age four until eighteen, but she lost her hearing due to a rare disease. She gave up music for a while, but discovered that she could not live without it. She was willing to try anything that might regain her connection with it, and along with that her sense of self-worth and value. So, she struggled through unimaginable challenges to find her voice and express herself and her passion for music even though she could no longer hear her own voice. Like Beethoven, who went deaf in his later years, she had to learn to feel the vibrations of her music through muscle memory and through her feet on the floor. Her performance on AGT had everyone on their feet with tears in their eyes. She said something in her introductory comments that I've never forgotten.

"After I lost my hearing, I just gave up," she said. "But I want to do more with my life than just give up." The audience was stunned into silence, and so were the judges. When she sang flawlessly an original song she wrote about not ever giving up, the audience went wild and gave her a standing ovation. That golden buzzer was one of the most well-deserved I've seen, although every one of them is precious. That's passion at its purest, and it's so inspiring I sometimes binge on compilations of the best performances for hours at a time just to keep myself inspired to never give up my own pursuit for excellence.

Passion is a calling of the soul – an awakening to something inside of us that wants to be experienced and developed to its fullest. When we sense that calling stirring in us, we often brush it aside as nonsense or something improbable or impractical. But when we pay attention to it, it pulls on us and drives us toward something unknown yet strangely familiar – a place, a goal or an unfulfilled dream. It forms a connection between imagination and creative spirit. It's a calling from deep in our psyche that offers opportunities to go beyond who and what we believe we are. Passion helps us believe in something beyond ourselves, and allows us to transcend the limited thinking that keeps us stuck in the mundane world, unable to move forward.

Late in the past century, the multi-billion-dollar Chrysler Corporation was on the verge of bankruptcy and thousands of jobs were at risk. Chairman Lee Iacocca singlehandedly saved the company by trusting his intuition that a new approach was needed and decided to go against popular thinking that "bigger was better." He completely changed Chrysler's approach to car design. Passion for innovation and success drove him to create a radical new approach to simplicity in car design, and the 'K' car came into being and saved the company.

During the post-WWII boom years, Air Force test pilot Chuck Yeager's passion for speed and pushing the proverbial envelope drove him to break the sound barrier in a crudely designed aircraft that was nothing more than a rocket with wings. Most "experts" were certain it couldn't be done. He went on from there to accomplish feats of daring that took him to the very edge of space. By the time NASA had its first success with sub-orbital manned space flight, Yeager had already been there twice in a rocket with a crude seat installed, and stubby wings. Passion drove him to do what others thought couldn't be done.

> *Passion is a calling of the soul – an awakening to something inside of you that wants to be experienced and developed to its fullest.*

Passion is accessible to anyone in any culture, any economic or social status, any age, gender, or country. It's not just for privileged people, or geniuses or the wealthy. Oprah Winfrey, J.K. Rowling, Bill Gates, Steve Jobs, and Elon Musk are only a few of the many people who have proven the ability of the human spirit, driven by passion, to accomplish feats beyond most people's imaginations. In almost every instance, each of them started at the bottom and survived dismal circumstances, yet persevered because their passion drove them to overcome the obstacles in their way.

Each of them awakened their passion and went beyond limitations that keep most people from accomplishing their full potential. Anyone can learn to listen to and trust their inner voice. Or not. You don't have to. You can just get by. There's nothing wrong with that. There's no doctrine or law or spiritual teaching that says you have to excel in life, or says that you're a failure if you don't. But inside each of us is an ability to grow, to evolve, to push ourselves to achieve our best. Until we find and cultivate passion, however, we don't know how to access the drive that it takes to push beyond our limited beliefs about ourselves, and our natural fear of failure that often stems from childhood trauma or perceived limitations.

Fear of failure keeps most of us stuck in our accepted daily routines, but those who push through that self-imposed barrier go for their dreams. For those who do, the possibilities of success are limitless, and are worth the potential risk of failure. Failure, most of them discover, is temporary and part of learning new ways of thinking and acting. They don't let that stop them from moving forward. Many of us carry the emotional scars from past failures and difficult experiences, and that blocks us from even trying. Although we can't change those experiences, we can change how we feel about them.

If we can change our thinking, and see our past mistakes and difficulties as opportunities to improve, we can turn fear into growth and self-expansion. Babe Ruth, best known as "The Home Run King" of the last century, was also known by his teammates as the "Strikeout King."

It's all a matter of perspective. Our success in life depends on whether we let our perceptions of ourselves limit us or drive us to overcome those limitations. Oprah Winfrey and J.K. Rowling, two of the world's most successful women, each faced poverty, abuse, and virtual homelessness at one point in their early beginnings. Bill Gates and Steve Jobs designed and perfected their computer operating systems in their garages, and both were turned down numerous times for investment capital. They weren't born into wealth, or possessed some secret skill or genius, yet they founded two of the most successful businesses in American history – Microsoft and Apple. Both admitted that at some point in their early years, they were each at a loss for what to do or how to move forward, but something drove them to keep going, keep innovating. That something was passion.

A very successful seminar leader I knew and worked with used a light bulb connected to a dimmer knob to illustrate a point about passion…or lack of it. As he described each incident in his life that had hurt him, or frightened him, he turned the dimmer down a little. As he spoke of being raised in a broken home, experiencing poverty, running away and being in trouble most of his young life, he turned it down some more. The light was so dim by the time he got to his early adulthood, it was barely visible. His point was further dramatized by the house lights being off during his talk so that by that point the room was nearly dark.

Then he described his eventual rise through various jobs and careers to become a ship captain, a Fortune 500 business trainer, and ultimately to one of the most successful personal growth seminar leaders in the country. As he spoke more positively about each accomplishment, he increased the light's intensity. "You've got to turn it *UP*," he would exclaim in an exuberant tone of voice, "and keep it up!" Then he wound the dimmer up to full brightness and the house lights came back up to emphasize his point.

"Life is difficult enough to manage with your light fully on," he said as he scanned the startled faces of his audience. "How can you expect to get through it with your light turned way down?"

Your "light" in this example is the symbol of your drive to succeed – to achieve the vision we're all born with that promises that we can do and be anything we want. You have to believe in that, or you will be like a hot air balloon tethered to the ground. The more attention you give to things that dim your light, the more dim your light will become. Conversely, the more time you spend with people doing things that amplify your light, the more passion you'll feel to achieve the vision you want for your life. It's a matter of choice, which is what this book is all about.

What's *your* passion? Do you think about it or wonder what it would take to accomplish something you really want but aren't sure how to do it? Do you feel something burning inside of you that keeps you restless and awake at night? Is something calling to you that you keep putting out of your thoughts because it's not related to anything you're presently doing, or feels too foolish, vague, or far away?

Is there a book you'd like write, or music you would like to sing or play? Are there certain people, places, clothes, or lifestyles that beckon to you from the pages of magazines, or in movies that make you feel like there's more to life than what you're experiencing? That's passion stirring inside of you of a future version of yourself waiting to be awakened. It doesn't matter who you are, where you come from or what you're doing. There are many stories of multi-millionaires who slept in their cars at some point in their lives. Steve Jobs dropped out of college after only six months, but stayed on for a year and a half and sat in on classes he wanted to take rather than the ones he was told he had to take. He slept on the floors and couches of his college friends' apartments and hitchhiked across town to get an occasional free meal at the Krishna Center in L.A. Those classes he unofficially took formed the basis for much of what went into his earliest operating systems, which led him to become one of the most successful business visionaries in history. By trusting his instincts rather than doing what was expected of him, he was able to create opportunities he otherwise never would have envisioned.

I read of a woman who became seriously ill with an auto-immune disorder, which was not well-known or understood even by medical experts at the time. She lost all motivation and physical strength with which to do anything, and at one point could barely get up off the floor. She had three children, and when her husband ultimately left her alone with the kids she was forced to do something different. Forced by circumstances to find the strength to look for a job, she managed to secure one as a receptionist at a large car dealership. Getting out of the house and having a job enabled her to gain some physical strength, and after a few weeks she began to feel better and more purposeful. As she watched salesmen on the showroom floor, she became inspired to sell cars and eventually talked the sales manager into letting her move to a sales position at a time when women were rarely seen doing that. Before long, she was the top salesperson for the dealership, and went on from there to eventually own two BMW dealerships. *True story…*

Overcoming a lifetime of limited thinking is not an easy thing. Just as old habits are hard to break, new habits are difficult to form and replace them. However, you are only limited by your own beliefs and fears. If you want to know what's inside you, and you're willing to put everything aside to achieve what you feel stirring there, start by listening and feeling more closely. Then read books on the subject. Seek out people, join online or community groups interested in the same subject, and find sources of information that fuel that desire and will pull on you to achieve your dreams.

I had the privilege of meeting a woman who was 5'2" tall and weighed barely 100 pounds. She grew up in Monterey, California, and had a passion to learn to fly long before women became airline pilots. She spent most of her spare time at the Monterey airport and did anything she could to be around pilots and airplanes. She got a job refueling planes, and eventually got her private license and gradually earned her commercial license. Then, a businessman whose Learjet she had often refueled found out she had a commercial license and was so impressed he hired her. When I met her, she was a full captain on "stretched" DC-8's for UPS...the largest and heaviest, commercial jet aircraft in use back then. She was a 5'2" powerhouse, and one of the most passionate people I knew.

> *Following your passion is a pursuit that will take you places you never thought possible. But you have to give it all you can.*

Following your passion is a pursuit that will take you places you never thought possible. But you have to give it all you can. It needs faith and determination to materialize, and perseverance to keep going. It doesn't matter if you don't know how to get there. Your desire and your vision of a better future means that you're listening, and your inner guidance will help you get there. That doesn't come from a textbook or an apprenticeship program. It comes from life itself, and an unyielding desire to excel and push beyond your perceived limitations. It's human nature.

Cheryl Richardson, author of *Finding Your Passion,* tells a story of an attorney struggling over his career choices. He went to law school, but he didn't really have a passion for law. So he got by with run-of-the-mill cases that paid the bills, but they didn't allow for the lifestyle he wanted. What he secretly yearned for was stand-up comedy, which he did as much as he could on the side. Not able to fully focus on either pursuit, he was mediocre at both until Cheryl advised him to abandon his law practice and throw himself totally into what he really wanted to do.

It was agonizing, according to Cheryl, for her to watch her good friend struggle over the next several months. New to standup comedy, he wasn't successful at first. She encouraged him to believe in himself so he stuck with it, gradually improved and eventually moved to L.A. where standup comedy was becoming fashionable. He was miserable at first, and several times almost gave up, but he slowly perfected his technique until he was "discovered" by a talent agent. In less than a year, he became a successful stand-up comedian making more than three times his attorney's income.

Passion requires one to be completely committed to their life's work. When Martin Luther King spoke his famous words, "I have a dream," there was no doubt that his heart, mind, and soul were committed to that dream. Whether people watched that speech in person, saw it on television or heard it on the radio, everyone knew what he stood for and that his whole life force was committed to it. He drew people into his world because of his passion for equality, and he affected not just a nation but an entire world.

Dr. King was not born an exceptional person, nor a privileged one. He came from humble beginnings and, living in pre-civil rights

America, had to work his way through many obstacles and violent resistance. He was no different, as he pointed out many times, than most Americans. But he had a burning passion for his cause. He was fully committed to it, and unwavering in his work to bring about his vision for a free society…for everyone.

When you look around at the people who influence your life, which ones inspire you the most? What do they do that stands out and stirs you to think differently? What parts of your work and life are exceptional or out of the ordinary? Are you stretching beyond your comfort zone by trying new things? Do you greet each day with a sense of eagerness and excitement, fully engaged with your life? Or are you just putting in your time and waiting for something to happen? If you don't feel like you're living the life you really want to live, and you feel stuck, try doing something different to shake things up. Keep it simple and just do small things at first, then take bigger steps. Ask yourself what you really want and stay still long enough to listen. Feel your inner guidance growing stronger and clearer. In time, with patience and practice, it will.

Passion is something that can only be accessed when you have the willingness and courage to step outside your comfort zone and reach for something greater. Passion takes purpose to a higher level of awareness. It's not something you can get out of books…even this one. It's a way of life…something you *become* by being unwilling to stay in the same place or keep doing the same things. It's something that requires your full attention, focus, and the willingness to let go of everything you thought was important. It requires that you trust the process and go for what lies deep in your heart as your foremost goal.

Our literature and movies are filled with stories of people caught in the trap of mediocrity, but who ultimately risk everything to discover the joys of living life more fully and passionately. It's worth everything, and your increasing success will inspire others to do the same. Conversely, if we allow others to impose their values and routines on us, we will never know the richness and power of who we truly are, nor will we ever discover what our vision for ourselves is or could have been. We give in, go numb and fall into mediocrity without ever realizing our destiny. We make excuses for the limitations we perceive we have, and we "get by."

Negative or positive, our thoughts are powerful. Coupled with purpose, vision and passion, thoughts are among the most powerful forces available to us. They make imagination become reality. We often hear it said that we are what we think we are. That means if we think we're unlucky with love, we'll keep attracting that. So it is also true that if we believe our lives are abundant, we will attract an abundance of positive situations, people, and opportunities.

Charles Yeates, a wealthy financier during the late 1800's, owned a great deal of property and bankrolled a large portion of the Chicago World Trade Exposition of 1893. At one point, Yeates suffered several severe political setbacks that threatened his financial ruin. With growing public awareness of the loss of his real estate wealth, his credibility plummeted…without which few people survived in that world. His circle of wealthy friends and associates diminished, thinking that he had little chance for a successful outcome.

Not a person to give in or give up, he understood the value of perception and how people act as a result, so he made a very bold move. He accepted a request from the University of Chicago to bankroll the construction of a new observatory for $300,000

($10,000,000 by todays standards), knowing that he had no real means to provide it. His condition was that it would take some time to "reposition" his funds, and that the observatory be named after him. When the news broke the next day, his credibility skyrocketed. Assuming that he must have some hidden wealth, banks competed with each other to lend him enough money to fund the observatory with enough left over to promote the Exposition, which attracted over twenty-six million people. Yeates had a colorful, even somewhat checkered past, but his passion was building things. He built and owned the Chicago trolley system, and was instrumental in developing the 600 acres needed for the Exposition that later became a cultural center of the city.

A more modern example of passion and determination is Ron Heagy, one of the most successful motivational speakers of our time. When Ron was about to turn eighteen, he was the quintessential All-American athlete – captain of the football team, 6'2", and could bench press 300 pounds. For his eighteenth birthday, he went on a surfing trip to Southern California.

On the morning before his birthday, Ron was living his dream, surfing on the sun-baked shores of Venice, CA when a sudden, rogue wave broke and jammed him headfirst into a sand bar and snapped his neck. When he woke up, he was in a hospital bed paralyzed from the neck down. The prognosis was grim, and for the next six months he suffered unspeakable mental and emotional trauma. There was no repairing the damage, and his slim hopes of recovery steadily evaporated. Unable to move any part of his body from the neck down, his hell became even worse. He wanted to die but he couldn't even blow his own nose without help, let alone take his own life.

Over time, he accepted that he wouldn't be able to do anything to change his grim circumstances. But the spark of human spirit couldn't be extinguished even under those circumstances. Ron felt determined to somehow improve his life. So, he started speaking publicly about his accident to bring visibility to those who suffered from spinal injuries, and that started a new path for him as the most inspiring motivational speaker I ever met. Ron's passion, if he couldn't be the best football player ever, was to become a beacon of hope for others who suffered similar injuries. He humorously said he decided he would be the "best paraplegic ever." He would pause to give the audience a moment to reflect on the irony of that statement, then he would say, "But then Christopher Reeves got thrown from a horse and suddenly I'm in competition with Superman." The audience roared with laughter, and from that point, he had them enraptured with his story.

About adversity, Ron says you only have two choices: you can make life better or worse by your daily choice of attitude and how passionately you pursue your dreams. For over forty years since his accident, he has made a lifetime passion of showing how one's choice of attitude makes all the difference, and enables one to achieve virtually any goal. Ron Heagy is married and has a daughter, paints masterful works of art with his teeth, and gives motivational talks all over the world. The unthinkable tragedy of his accident and the immensity of his personal challenge is what cultivated his true passion and purpose in life – to use his life to inspire others to find their purpose and passion.

Passion is not just an esoteric notion, and it's never too late. Harlan Sanders was seventy-three when a new freeway re-routed commercial traffic away from his restaurant, so he took his secret recipe and his skill, know-how, and passion to Lexington, Kentucky, and Kentucky Fried Chicken, now a global commercial empire, was born.

We're here for a reason that's greater than just making it from cradle to grave. A good friend of mine sent me an email once that said, "Life isn't meant to be lived perfectly preserved and protected, but rather to be lived fully and passionately such that one comes sliding into the grave, scarred and tattered, drink in hand, exclaiming "Wow! What a ride!"

How do you find your passion? Feel for what you most love to do. Cultivate your passion by doing more of it, and seeking out others who share a similar desire for it. Make your ride one that's worth living. Stay inspired…not just motivated. Do what you came here to do by spending the rest of your life finding out what that is, and learning all you can about it, like the 5'2" DC-8 captain. Never stop learning. It will make your life bigger, better and bolder than anything else you could possibly do. The possibilities are limitless.

> *"Whatever you can do or dream you can do, begin it NOW! Boldness has genius, power and magic in it."*
>
> – Goethe

"If you have the courage to begin, you have the courage to succeed."

— Harry Hoover

CHAPTER FOUR
Courage

A classic line in the Declaration of Independence essentially says that when something is wrong with our government, those who are strong enough have not only a right but a responsibility to do something about it. Those are very powerful words, but it's going to take a lot more than words to do something about what's going on in the world today. Above all, it's going to take courage…and a lot of it.

Our country's Founding Fathers were overthrowing a government that was abusive and uncaring. They put their lives on the line, and risked everything for freedom to live according to their principles and a democratic form of government. I'm not suggesting we overthrow anything but rather take a meaningful stand for principled ways of living and governing ourselves. This is not a political statement. I'm neither Democrat nor Republican. I'm an American…first and foremost. Moreover, I'm a human being, and I'm taking a stand for moral and rightful equality of everyone on the planet. What I'm saying is that each of us, no matter who we are, must do whatever we can to see that all people are treated with respect and decency, and make certain that our leaders do also. Even if it seems small and insignificant, everything of a positive and caring nature adds up and contributes to the whole scheme of things for our near and long-term future. I believe that's what our forefathers had in mind in 1776, and a democracy was formed that laid the groundwork for a country that has endured some of the most difficult times in modern history.

Since then, things have gotten out of balance because we haven't paid attention to how things are being managed and, all too often, manipulated to benefit the few on the inside under the guise of "national interests" or "security." As one of our 2020 Presidential candidates pointed out during the debates, "We've gone to sleep as a nation and as a society. We've lost track of who we are, and how important it is for each of us to pay closer attention to who is running the show."

That "show" needs some serious redirecting for all the reasons I'm writing about in these chapters. To do that is going to take a wake-up call not only on the part of the American people, but gradually on all of humanity…but that's what may be happening right now. I know that's a pretty tall order, but so was the American Revolution. The colonists were way outnumbered and overpowered and, like we are in 2021, they were divided between the new way of thinking and loyalty to the old, established way that was controlled by the rich and powerful. It took courage for those who believed in self-governance, even if it looked hopeless that they could prevail. *But eventually they did*…because it was morally right to do so, and in the common interests of the people. In doing so, they established a whole new form of government that has lasted over 200 years. That government was based on common human decency and the right of men (and later, women) to govern themselves. Of course, there was the slavery issue to be resolved, and women's rights, and other issues that would grow in significance, but at least the framework of self-governance, freedom and independence had been outlined and established. There would be no turning back. That's what is needed today, and may be exactly what's happening around the globe. We need to get back on track in no weak or hesitant way, and what we're dealing with economically, socially and politically now should be ample reason to create a whole new track in a very different direction.

This is not a right or wrong posture I'm suggesting. It's not an attack on the rich and powerful, or a political issue. It's a fundamental principal of morality and equal rights for all…not just a few. Everyone has their place, and no one should be restricted or disregarded or dismissed based upon gender, culture, class or ethnicity. Everyone should have a right to improve and be heard and allowed to take part in deciding on matters that impact our futures and the futures of our children and their children.

Among the many barriers preventing us from getting ourselves back on that track, or on a whole new track, are limiting beliefs, old behavior patterns, and fear-based thinking that I've mentioned previously, but to take it deeper, let's consider fear. Fear is at the core of most of our social and behavioral problems. From childhood we learn fear of all types: fear of strangers, fear of the dark, of failing in school, rejection by our peers, authorities, and so forth, until by the time we reach adulthood we are virtually paralyzed by fear about everything. Rigidified by habit patterns growing up, we develop fears of losing our jobs, our health, taking risks, getting old, loneliness, financial ruin, and so on. Such fears influence our everyday lives to the point where we will say anything, do anything, or believe anything that even appears likely to relieve the anxieties, stress and discomforts of these turbulent times.

Our language tells the story of our lives and the virtual paralysis that many of us feel increasing by the day. Listen closely to what people say, and listen to yourself as well. If you're attentive, you will increasingly come to realize that people...even you...are scared to death. We're still in the throes of a global pandemic, which still threatens half the world's population. Now we're dealing with the realities of that every day. But it's really not things, people, or circumstances that cause fear. The pandemic is certainly real, but it's our own feelings of inadequacy and lack of understanding what causes our fears that keeps us afraid and unable to deal with all the challenges and uncertainties we face.

> *Our language tells the story of our lives and the virtual paralysis that many of us feel increasing by the day.*

One important realization that came to me in my thirties when I was still young enough to change habit patterns, was discovering how accepting responsibility for my circumstances enabled me to save myself from more serious trouble later. But as time passed, I also discovered that accepting responsibility wasn't enough. It also required that I be willing to "own" it – meaning accepting that I created it and must be willing to tell the truth about it. That's a whole different thing. Doing that opens up extraordinary dynamics in one's life, including "working miracles" that I've referred to several times in this book. That's because "owning" means that you accept that you created it, and therefore you have the power to create something better with what you have learned because of it.

I unwittingly put this new realization to the test in no small way when I had the opportunity to meet face to face with my own federal prosecutor when I was in prison awaiting trial. At the most critical moment in that entire journey, I was able to tell him what happened without incriminating anyone else. I could have held back out of fear that he was laying a trap for me, or danced around the issues, but I didn't do any of that. I just had to speak my own truth about my involvement in a crime so he could better understand my motives to confirm what he already surmised from reading my files. If I had withheld anything, blamed someone else, or denied any of the facts, the meeting would have been over and I would have done some serious time. I didn't know that he was actually giving me an opportunity to turn things around. I was a decent person who had made some foolish choices, but I was on the brink of becoming a career inmate. In that critical moment, I made a choice and took a risk by telling the truth. That decision put me on a different and better path to a brighter future. It could have cost me that future.

As I travel around the country and listen to people's stories, now as a free man rather than on prison buses and the real "Con-Air," I'm saddened at how fearful and angry people are. Many are generally either withdrawn and feeling helpless and victimized, or they are overly concerned with pleasing each other because they fear being rejected, denied, and alone. Seldom does anyone actually say what they mean and speak the truth about their real feelings. Speaking the truth takes courage.

The media – visual, print and online – fills our heads with compelling notions of how we should live, or what kind of homes, cars, and clothes present successful images. Formal education teaches us academic skills to train our minds. Employment helps us develop good work ethics. But where do we learn how to deal with life ethically and courageously, how to be free-thinking, independent people? And where do we learn how to take risks? Instead, we learn to conform…to go along with the images we learn growing up. In the process, we lose track of our own value and of the value of each human being. How ironic that our country was founded on the principles of freedom and independence, yet very little of that is actually taught in our schools or at home. We have lost track of who we are and what our lives are worth.

> *The one root cause of all our fears is that (we) don't matter. We fear that we have no real value in life or to others.*

Therein lies the greatest fear of all: that we don't matter or have value. Rabbi Jacob Boteach, in his book *Face Your Fear,* writes, "The one root cause of all our fears is that (we) don't matter. We fear that we have no real value in life or to others. To be afraid," he adds, "is to be reduced from a human being of destiny to a creature with no future." By that, he didn't mean that you can't be afraid, but rather not to be controlled or intimidated by fear.

Fear is pervasive in our society, and is as contagious and emotionally debilitating as any physical disease or malady. In fact, fear has been tied to physical illness, depression, heart disease and even cancer. It causes people to say things and do things that are not what they really intended. Along with physical illness, fear can bring about emotional and mental paralysis, even trauma.

Prisons are filled with men, women, and children (minors) who are there not so much because they broke laws but because they were so heavily influenced and controlled by their fears, they made choices that were irrational and contrary to what many of them really wanted in life. I know. I was one of them. I spent a great deal of time with inmates from all cultures, backgrounds, and attitudes who were living products of the ravages of fear. Without exception, those who were honest with me admitted that the patterns of fear-based thinking started when they were children, and it was always exacerbated by feeling they had no way to deal with those fears.

I see the same patterns outside of prisons, too. Sometimes it's more glaring on the outside because of the invisible masks people wear – doing or saying things that don't match their true intent. I hear it in their voices and see it in the manner with which people conduct their businesses and their lives. Hardly anyone tells the full and real truth about things, or keeps their word. But even so, I'm optimistic and hopeful. I think most people really want that kind of clarity, decency and honesty.

Life doesn't have to be so fear-driven and influenced by doubt and resistance. That's all learned behavior and peer pressure. In my humble opinion, the majority of us weren't born that way...not even so-called "hardened criminals." Having been in prison, I can attest to the fact that fear was at the root of most behavior of those with whom I spoke. Innately, we are not "bad" or "evil." Our fears make us that way. Given enough fear, threats and hostility, most people will take the course of least resistance and discomfort. They give in, and fade into the most accepted way of thinking and acting. To live in constant fear, take short cuts and make excuses is a choice. Living authentically and speaking your truth is also a choice. We can choose to work hard, build new habits, and create positive change. Creating better attitudes, which I address in the next chapter, and changing our thinking and behavior enables people to "rewire" themselves and create new scripts, as I learned to see it later on in my journey. But it takes time and repeated efforts to make them lasting and automatic.

We all have a fundamental freedom, regardless of our past, our mistakes, traumas, and current life circumstances. That freedom is our choice of attitude at any point along the path of our lives. Over that, we have total control, no matter where our previous choices have taken us. When I wrote in Chapter One that, "something has to give," I could have been referring to a wide range of things, from municipal politics to worldwide economic collapse and global warming. Certainly our experience with 9/11 represents massive, global hostility and imbalance, all stemming from collective fear of the most severe kind since Pearl Harbor and every other war or military conflict of the past century. But there is something else far more elemental that shapes our attitude toward each other, and about ourselves. That is our ability to choose our attitude, and that takes courage.

Changing our attitude is a personal shift that has vast potential for positive change. If enough people start thinking and acting differently towards themselves and toward each other, the ripple effect around the globe could be substantial. It could positively impact American foreign relations, for one thing. It could improve the environment and the health of our planet. Everything and everyone is affected by how we think and act toward one another. That doesn't mean embracing or agreeing with anyone else's philosophy or behavior, but rather being willing to hear others' points of view and respecting their existence and value.

To respect someone doesn't mean agreeing with, or even liking them. It simply means we suspend our judgments and resistance enough to allow for differences between us, creating the possibility that any individual might have something to contribute to our lives. Apart from the most basic needs for physical survival, the greatest need we have as individuals is to feel as if we matter to others. To listen to someone is among the greatest gifts we can give. Listening validates their existence, and in as short a time as it takes to stand in a grocery store checkout line and greet someone with respect, you can literally change someone's life…and yours in the process.

Acts of kindness are another form of courage. Groups of inmates have donated thousands of dollars and untold hours of volunteer time assisting victims of forest fires, floods, and other national disasters. Muslim clerics have shown respect and support for American schools and other public institutions by approving the display of Christmas lights, Nativity scenes, and other Christian-based holiday decorations, despite how these customs may differ from their own faith. That's respect. It's not a position of weakness. It demonstrates strength and courage because it's proactive choice instead of reactive posturing.

The practice of respect allows for another person to feel or believe as they wish. If that person breaks the law or breaches established rules of ethical behavior, they compromise that respect. But our willingness to be objective and suspend judgment allows them to correct their mistakes. We all make mistakes. Condemnation and demeaning reactions only complicate and amplify the circumstances and ignores the causes, resulting in those mistakes often leading to bitterness and resentment, and hardened attitudes. To change such attitudes is essential not only to restoring our individual honor, but to our growth and survival as a society. That will not be easy for most people. Lifetimes of negative behavior and limiting beliefs are difficult but not impossible to change. It takes a great deal of personal courage to look at ourselves objectively and bring about the changes we each need to make because change requires more honesty and directness than most of us are willing to admit or accept. We've learned to mistrust the unfamiliar, avoid people we don't know, and appease those from whom we want recognition and acceptance. Most of these behaviors are automatic and unconscious.

Courage begins with being willing to tell the truth, all the time, every day…and to tell it "faster and better," as a wise woman once told me. She constantly pointed out things I said that weren't entirely truthful, but rather to her were only attempts to appease others rather than speaking authentically. I felt certain I was being truthful so I didn't like hearing this from her. But I cared enough about her opinion and wisdom to listen rather than react. I trusted that she was trying to help me. As I began to appreciate her raw, even brutal honesty, I gradually caught myself doing it. Sometimes I'd get it in mid-thought and could "course-correct" before the words came out of my mouth. Other times, if I didn't catch them in time, I would stop talking in mid-sentence, back up, and re-phrase what I was trying to say. I soon discovered that people appreciate the courage it takes to tell the truth, even if they don't appear to at first. Saying what we truly mean disarms people, and breaks down walls of misperception and misunderstanding.

As a salesman and promoter for most of my adult life, I learned at an early age that success depends on skillful persuasiveness. The better we are at it, the more we are praised for it as a virtue. It can be highly misleading, however, because most people don't want to be "sold" anything, no matter what it is. They may subconsciously want what you have to offer, but they don't want to be *sold* or convinced of anything. If your intentions are clear and honest, people will co-operate with you *and* feel good about it. This takes a great deal of personal courage and willingness to do some up-close and objective self-examination, then to apply what you discover to your daily activities.

A very wise friend of mine told me once about the energy of words. He said words carry a certain energy that changes with different usages and purposes, but beneath them is the vibration of your intention, which acts as a "carrier" of those words. If the vibration of your words doesn't match the vibration of your intention, the message you convey feels out of synch. People may go along with you, but down deep they won't really trust you. They'll feel something is off. That's the meaning of the phrase "bad vibes." The vibration you're giving off might not be necessarily bad, just a mismatch or imbalance in energy. The words are one message, but the vibe of the carrier is another.

> *Words carry a certain energy that changes with different usages and purposes, but beneath them is the vibration of your intention, which acts as a "carrier" of those words.*

In the movie, *Gladiator*, the Roman general Maximus walks down the line of officers and soldiers preparing for battle with Mongol hordes, and exchanges a motto with each of his commanders. Each of them, in turn, does the same with each of their troops until everyone has been acknowledged. The motto is "Strength and Honor." Each time they are uttered, there is an increase in the strength and intensity of the words as they are conveyed until it reaches the back ranks, when its full force is clear, unified and palpable. As I watched each exchange, I felt the sense of unification building until it was overwhelming. Even though it was just a movie, it was an inspiring demonstration of the power of the human spirit when aligned with something greater than ourselves when we're aligned with each other. In that example, the words and the carrier aligned and then intensified because it expanded across an entire army.

Strength and honor are not just words, nor are they merely for soldiers on the battlefield. They are what courage is all about. On the battlefield of human interactions, the courage to tell the truth, to *reveal ourselves,* will transform us. You don't have to be a general of troops or a Martin Luther King or Gandhi to inspire others and make an impact. Just inspire a few other people in your life to live more courageously, more honestly and more thoughtfully, and they will have the same effect on others. Before long, we may see a massive shift in global consciousness. It's already happening now, bit by bit. If you apply it daily in your own life, you will notice it with others, and you will become more sensitive to it.

Try it. Inspire one other person and see what comes of it. Then another, and another. You inspire others by setting an example. By encouraging others, and recognizing and acknowledging them for something they did, you can make a difference in the world. Give it some time and stay open to whatever comes back around to you. It can be very subtle at first, but if you're patient and observant, a pattern of good things will happen for you. When I was in prison, several of us experimented with this process, and the results were undeniably positive. In one instance, we tried it on the most offensive and dislikeable inmate. He was so surprised by inmates suddenly greeting him pleasantly that he gradually became more pleasant. Attitudes toward him began to change among inmates who weren't even part of the experiment. We saw and felt an entirely different attitude in him and toward others…even the guards.

It starts with you and me. You can positively impact the people around you, one at a time. It will take courage to face your fears, to embrace an attitude of self-forgiveness and then forgiveness of others. By taking a stand for yourself and extending that to respect others without judging them, you can create change you never thought was possible. That takes courage of a different kind, but no less powerful and lasting than Maximus and his motto, "Strength and Honor."

With *that,* we can indeed change the world…and change with it as we do.

*"The ones who are crazy enough
to think that they can
change the world,
are the ones who do."*

— Steve Jobs

CHAPTER FIVE

Attitude

Except for air, water and food, there are few things more important than attitude. Your attitude defines, molds, and shapes who you are and how you make your way in the world. It even determines your state of health because how you look at life directly impacts your immune system by either enhancing or depleting your vital energy. If you are constantly angry, mean-spirited, bitter, or depressed, your state of health will be adversely affected. You can count on that. There are numerous books, movies, documentaries and TED Talks that have well-established this as a fact. A negative attitude will drive away things that can help overcome physical, emotional or mental challenges, and chances are such a person won't eat right, exercise right, or maintain a healthy lifestyle.

Conversely, if you are strong, positive, grateful and good-natured, you will attract people and circumstances that will encourage you and help you build on that attitude. I think of a positive attitude as a form of healthcare. Positive-minded intentions and interactions attract the same types of interactions. Why? Because a positive, caring and optimistic attitude empowers one with resources that aren't available to people with negative and pessimistic attitudes. In short, a negative attitude attracts negative results, and a positive attitude attracts positive people and circumstances that will improve one's outlook on life and their future.

You can survive in life with a bad attitude by sheer willpower and stubbornness, but you will never really be truly successful. Attitude determines who we are, how we interact with the world around us and what types of experiences we draw into our lives. No matter how strong, smart, wealthy or powerful one may become, ultimately their attitude determines the quality of their life beyond just the quality of their material possessions.

> *You can survive in life with a bad attitude by sheer willpower and stubbornness, but you will never really be truly successful.*

I read a poster once that said "A hundred years from now, it won't matter what kind of car you drove, what kind of clothes you wore or how much money you had in the bank. The only thing that will matter is whether you made a difference in the life of a child." I've amended that to "…in the lives of others," because it applies equally well to everyone. While I believe that both are true, it's also true that you really can't make much of a positive impact on anyone's life with a bad attitude. A good attitude is fundamental to life as we know it. We love our heroes and our champions, our gold medal-winning athletes, and award-winning movie stars, but the people who really make lasting impressions on us are those who do things that unselfishly benefit others.

It's easy to be caught up in the complexities of making a living, paying the rent or mortgage, and creating stability for our families. To develop successful careers, we often find that we need to compromise our values to make our way up the ranks. We go through our daily routines at work and in life with steadily decreasing enthusiasm because we're too focused on acquiring material things and impressing others. When things go wrong, people often blame the circumstances or other people instead of considering their part in having created the situation. When they go really wrong, as in my journey through the federal prison system, we are lost for a logical or safe way out of the mess. We scramble to find any way to fix the problem, and often only make things worse. I certainly did…until I applied principles like right attitude no matter what things looked like or felt like to me.

On that note, I must point out that with few exceptions, it's never too late. Depending upon how long it takes you to correct the situation or circumstances you have created for yourself, a positive and open attitude will eventually turn things around. It may take longer than you wish, and more effort than you might care to expend, but I can assure you that it's well worth it. As Walt Disney supposedly said, "Success is getting up one more time than you are knocked down." If that's true – and I believe it is – then it's especially so when you come to realize that the only one who "knocked you down" is yourself.

Solutions come in many different forms, and they may appear differently than you expect or wish. But when you start paying close enough attention, and cultivate a positive attitude, you'll discover how small changes in how you think and act bring positive results. This showed up repeatedly for me in my prison experience. What I learned from Big Jim, my prison mentor, about finding something to be grateful for every day stayed with me throughout the many moves and twelve different facilities I was in. To most of the other inmates and officers, I was just a "skinny, smart-ass white guy," and easy prey. But as I learned to listen more and become more observant, I noticed a different attitude among many of them. My respectful attitude without appearing to "suck up" to or appease anyone seemed to give them reason to pause and wonder about me. Gradually, I took on the air of confidence I learned from Big Jim. Combined with my practice of gratitude, it brought amazing results. But they didn't come right away…just gradually as I managed to make a habit of listening more and observing my impact on others.

    The quiet contemplation involved in watching sunsets has been a constant source of inspiration in my life. I've found that slowing down long enough to appreciate nature is a good way to cultivate a positive attitude. Victor Frankl wrote about how gratitude worked for him and others in Nazi concentration camps by pausing while working in the snow to watch sunrises, and being grateful simply to be alive in the midst of horrific circumstances. They were grateful for the love they felt for their families, which was true even though few of them knew if they were even still alive. In spite of that, they found solace and some measure of peace in such simple things when others were understandably consumed by fear of dying at any moment. This attitude obviously had a positive result in the fact that most of them survived their entire time in what came to be known as the "death camps" that 6,000,000 people did not survive.

    In my own time in confinement, I had a job at the prison bakery that had me up at 3:00 a.m. each day, when all the gladiators and troublemakers were asleep. I recalled that story from Frankl's book, and since my work was done by six, I would often go outside and stand at a permissible distance from the fences and watch the sun come up each day. Frankl was right. Those peaceful few minutes each morning gave me a deep remembrance of loved ones on the outside, and this evoked such gratitude in me that it calmed my nerves and gave me an inner sense of acceptance and contentment. The more that attitude grew in me, the more it had a noticeable impact on other aspects of my life and, gradually, on fellow inmates. Later, when I was moved to another facility and wasn't allowed outside because I was "in transit," I was able to watch sunsets through a narrow, vertical window. I came to cherish those moments of serene beauty in the midst of dismal circumstances. I imagined people in opposite parts of the world watching the same sun rising, and recalled an evening prayer I had read once that gave me solace and reason to look forward to the next morning: *"Thank you for the joy of living today, in the spirit of beauty, goodness, and kindness. May joy and gratitude radiate in other parts of the world, as the sun disperses the night and brings the joy of the day."*

To this day, I still pause when I notice a sunset and remember that prayer.

The sense of inner freedom that came to me as each day turned slowly into night outside that narrow window calmed me and gave me a sense of hope and promise that someday soon I would be out there again, free to watch sunsets and sunrises of my own free will whenever I wanted to. It made all my other concerns seem small and temporary. The time spent in solitary confinement was scary at first, but gradually I saw that it was good for me to have time alone. I felt gratitude building inside of me again, as I did not have to maintain a defensive posture or alertness among rowdy and confrontational inmates. I was grateful to be in good health and able to reason my way through a great deal of trouble and uncertainty. By the time I was allowed out into the general prison population, I realized I had cultivated a new sense of peace with my circumstances. I felt more confident and empowered. My time in solitary confinement and my practice of gratitude helped me communicate in more sensitive ways with the hostile inmates, which gradually inspired some of them to want to improve their lives. By focusing on gratitude and cultivating a sense of peace within myself, I was able to shift my obsession from my own personal plight to assisting others in improving theirs.

Small groups and eventually small classes of inmates came together for me to work with and, unbeknownst to me as my influence grew, comments and letters of commendation appeared in my files. The positive impact expanded from there, even to officers and staff who were merely observers of our activities. What appeared to be a hopeless situation and a possible twenty-five year sentence became eight years, and I was released in just over two and a half years' total time served.

Later, when I wrote my first book about the experience, the prosecutor in my case was so impressed with my continued work on the outside that he agreed to write the Foreword for my first book. The irony of his original determination to see me behind bars for the rest of my adult life, and now having become a friend and ally was immense. It was also another thing for which to be hugely grateful. After the book was completed, he even consented to appear in a heartwarming, videotaped testimonial for me to present at a large annual conference of correctional and law enforcement officers that launched my work in prison and social justice reform.

My vivid imagination while in prison often had me awake late at night, imagining coming back to prison a free man in the future to speak to inmates about how to deal with incarceration, and preparing for their eventual return to society. Never did I imagine I would be a keynote speaker at an annual forum of correctional and law enforcement officers – including wardens, judges, and prosecutors – and treated with respect and admiration. After the close of that talk, a well-dressed man approached me and shook my hand. I could tell by the way the other officials treated him that he must be important, but with me he was so casual I felt an instant sense of mutual admiration and friendship. He said what I had spoken about was something he had wanted to institute in "his facilities" for years. We talked uninterrupted for twenty minutes when the warden of the prison came up to him.

> *(Positive) attitude opened doors I would never have seen or known about if my attitude had been anything less.*

"I'm sorry to interrupt you, Mr. Secretary," the man spoke hesitantly, "but we have a meeting to attend." Only then did I realize that I had been speaking casually with the Secretary of Corrections, the top correctional official for the State of Washington, as if we were colleagues. Me, whose only credentials were having served time in the federal prison system and wrote a book about it, and he treated me as an equal. Later, the warden took me on a personal tour of the entire facility, which completed my vision years before imagining I would someday tour prisons as a free man and someone who could do something positive to change attitudes on both sides of the fences and walls.

Attitude allowed that to happen. I'm living proof that a determined and respectful attitude opens doors left and right...doors I would never have seen or known about if my attitude had been anything less. A few months later, I was in that same Secretary's office laying out plans for the development of a series of workshops to be conducted in his biggest state prison as a pilot program to eventually extend to his other facilities. He authorized me to speak regularly to all inmates at another facility that handled all the incoming and processing of new inmates for the entire state of Washington, so I could help instill a positive attitude on the part of the inmates as well as the staff and officers.

What I discovered along the way was that you can mask your feelings but you can't hide your attitude for long because one way or another the authenticity of how you feel comes across. These were the highest-ranking officials in the Washington State Correctional system, all of them experts in dealing with the worst and most manipulative inmates. Most of them had seen it all, having worked their way up through the ranks from fledgling correctional officers. There is no way I could fake or manipulate my way into their confidence. The ironies of where I had been and where I was then were a powerful reminder that a consistently positive attitude will open doors for you that you never knew existed.

Your attitude about yourself, about others, and about life will reveal itself in many ways. If it's positive, it will shine through your daily affairs in the form of good luck, breakthroughs, positive affirmations and chance encounters that will change your life. I can personally attest to not a few but many events that were nothing short of miraculous. On the other hand, if it's negative, it will show up in the form of illness, irritation, stress or misfortune.

The quality of our relationships and interactions tell us a lot about our attitude as they are reflected back to us. If you feel good about yourself, people will feel good about you and you will attract other people with positive attitudes. If someone treats you badly, you might contemplate how they might be responding to something you said or did unknowingly. The same woman who reminded me to be truthful and authentic also said something I've never forgotten. "No matter how good a communicator you think you are," she said rather matter-of-factly, "the only thing that really matters is how it lands on their plate." Once again, she was right, no matter how logically or righteously I could protest. I've noticed it again and again since then, and have been able to correctly gauge how my words might "fall on others' plates," and it has made all the difference in the world to me as I speak with or write to others.

Considering the attitude you hold toward yourself is the first step in cultivating positive attitudes about others and the world around you. What practices do you engage in that will improve your health and well-being? Do you exercise or practice yoga? Do you spend quiet time in nature contemplating or meditating? Self-nurturing activities like those will cultivate a deeper practice of self-care, and will build a positive attitude about yourself and your intrinsic value, your capabilities, and your willingness to cultivate self-care.

It's also helpful to know that the greatest gift we can give anyone, no matter how briefly or how long we know them, is to show that we value them. Starting by valuing ourselves gives even more substance to that practice. We all want to know that we matter to others. If your attitude is open and caring, and if you communicate honestly and clearly, others will feel your respect and will want to interact with and know more about you.

Big Jim overcame challenges you can't even imagine. By changing his attitude toward his tormentors, he turned the tables on them and came out of prison with a good job, self-respect and a healthy outlook, even though it took twenty years. His attitude change was a conscious choice, and it set him free under the worst, most horrendous conditions imaginable. I was lucky to have been the recipient of his advice during the brief time we were together. The lesson he taught me about the power of right attitude enabled me to experience the same sense of personal freedom that's alive in me today.

> *We keep ourselves imprisoned or free by our choice of attitude every day that we get up by what we choose to believe about ourselves and others.*

We keep ourselves imprisoned or free by our choice of attitude every day that we get up by what we choose to believe about ourselves and others. I see it on the faces of people doing things they think others can't see or notice. This is especially true while they're driving in their cars. They don't realize that people can see their faces quite readily, and oftentimes they aren't pleasant or pretty. I've seen more people outside of prison locked up and trapped in negative and limiting beliefs than I saw inside of them.

The way to avoid the subtle prison of limiting beliefs and create a feeling of personal freedom is to pay attention to how you show up for other people. Do your interactions with others make them feel as if they matter to you? Do you act as if you truly value others, or are just giving them lip service while you wait to say what you want to say? You don't have to agree with them, but you can certainly suspend judgment and offer a kind word, a common courtesy, or even a warm smile. Real human connection comes in many forms. It can be small and insignificant, yet still be life-changing to many people.

You can put these small changes into action through everyday activities. For example, give other motorists a chance to enter traffic ahead of you on a busy street. The simplest things can change others' outlook and attitude, and nothing improves attitudes like feeling respected and appreciated. Willingness to look within and be more respectful toward others can change the world. It begins with each of us.

It won't cost you a thing but the time and effort needed to change your point of view, and your attitude. And then patience and trust while others change theirs. It takes time to change life-long perspectives and attitudes.

*"Truth is ever to be found
in simplicity, and not
in the multiplicity and confusion
of things."*

– Isaac Newton

CHAPTER SIX

Truth

In the movie, *Excalibur*, after all the battles had been fought and won, King Arthur and his knights gather to celebrate their victories and honor their brotherhood. At one point, as they are extolling the victories and the establishment of Camelot, Arthur raises his hand and the room quiets. When all eyes are on him, he asks, "What say each of you is a knight's greatest virtue?"

"Bravery," says one.

"Nobility," offers another.

"Loyalty," says the next.

"Courage" says another, and everyone robustly agrees that it is the greatest.

Merlin, the king's mentor since childhood, stands quietly by the wall, listening. When the last one speaks, he rolls his eyes and turns toward the door to leave, but Arthur stops him.

"O' great Merlin, what say thee? What is a knight's greatest virtue?"

A hush falls over the room as Merlin turns and peers fiercely at each knight, one at a time. The silence is palpable.

"Truth, my Lord," he finally proclaims. He pauses to allow the full impact to be weighed in each mind, then he continues. "Without truth, there is no point to bravery or nobility. Without truth, there is no value to loyalty or honor." He pauses again, then peers directly at Arthur. "It is my belief, Sire, that with every lie, no matter how small, something in the universe dies." He nods respectfully, turns and leaves the room.

I've thought about that scene many times over the years, and I've watched and felt for how it has played out in my interactions with others. It may have only been a scene in a movie, but something about it rings true. If I'm honest with myself, I know that whenever I've lied or even slightly twisted the truth, I feel a sense of loss and emptiness form in my mind. It's an uneasiness, like one senses when the flickering light of a candle blows out in the darkness of night. With that lie, or even an omission of something true, comes some sense of loss. I can feel it, and I believe the recipient can feel it as well.

> *Lying may be the greatest form of disrespect because you are telling that person that they don't matter.*

Lying may be the greatest form of disrespect because by lying to someone you are essentially telling them that they don't matter, even if the lie was intended to protect them. While they may never discover the untruth, you know that you've disrespected them by misrepresenting something or holding something back.

A lie is a bad seed planted in one's psyche. Until it's uprooted and replaced with the truth, it carries the energy of something invasive that can grow and spread like a weed. Even if you're never found out, *you* know it's there, and the energy of that deception stays in your subconscious no matter how deeply you may bury it. Added to that is always the possibility that your lie may be discovered. When and if that happens, then you're in worse trouble than whatever the lie was meant to cover. The only course to take if that happens is to own it without sidestepping or rationalizing, to offer a meaningful, genuine apology and repair the damage as best you are able to. It might take a while to heal, so no side-stepping if you value that person in your life.

An omission, intentional or otherwise, has essentially the same effect as a lie. If it's someone you're close to, they will very likely sense you're withholding something. The "vibe" of your omission creates a feeling of doubt or uncertainty between you, which eventually leads to suspicion and distrust. They'll sense that something's not quite right, even though you might come off sincere and trustworthy. The fact something's being withheld creates a feeling of evasiveness and discomfort that often leads to the very outcome you are trying to avoid…or worse. I've experienced it again and again, even at the smallest level. Trouble is, there's really nothing "small" about it, even if both people brush it off as a "white lie." It's always there in each other's awareness. When and if something of a similar nature comes up, it will rear its ugly head.

But there's good news. With courage and honesty, the damage can be repaired. Admitting to a lie – even an omission – takes courage and honesty because trust has been compromised. Restoring that trust can be a long and challenging process, but has many rewards. Trust can be rebuilt. If there is true sincerity and remorse, relations can become stronger than ever as long as it isn't repeated.

Sometimes we don't realize we're lying if our intention is to justify or rationalize an action. These practices have become so commonplace they permeate our entire world of commerce, marketing, and advertising. In many ways, this has become the way people communicate in the business world – misrepresenting or twisting the truth, or omitting important details in a way that is so accepted it doesn't feel wrong. Seldom do the ends justify the means if the means are based on mistruths. Things get murky, and at some point truth becomes indistinguishable from lies. The more successful one becomes, and is praised for it, the harder it is to stop and consider what's really occurring. This happens most often in politics, where so much is on the line and the media gets involved. Lying, in some form, becomes the standard default behavior and an accepted standard. No one even questions it if it's the prevailing belief.

The late President Richard Nixon, architect of the infamous Watergate scandal, epitomized this disconnection from the truth, as dramatically illustrated in his interview with renowned British journalist David Frost. At one point deep into the interview, Frost skillfully maneuvered Nixon into a cathartic realization of how far he had deviated from truth and integrity. The moment was captured for all the world to see when Nixon unwittingly admitted he had allowed himself to believe that if he could convince enough people with the power of his office and his cleverly structured rhetoric, then he hadn't really done anything wrong. It was a colossal act of justification, and a breathtaking admission, amplified and dramatized by his sudden silence as his face turned visibly ashen. He was suddenly lost for words, and unable for several moments to even speak coherently. In this striking disclosure, the truth he'd been evading for years finally revealed itself even to him, and provided invaluable incentive for all of us to re-think and reflect on how we engage with others.

I was a born salesman and was trained to think that salesmanship was a virtue like some kind of Olympic victory or oratory accomplishment. I was often praised for being adept at convincing people they needed whatever I had to offer. No matter what it was – cutlery, pots and pans, tires, fire alarms, cars, or a business concept, I could sell it. I learned to say what needed to be said, and even though I believed much of what I said was true, all too often I got caught up in making the sale rather than feeling for the truth of what I was selling.

Many of the young women of that time period to whom such things as hope chests were an important part of growing up, I was able to convince that what I had to offer was a must-have part of their future. Many of them worked at low-income jobs trying to get by, and didn't need and couldn't really afford a lifetime set of cutlery or dishes or pots and pans. It hardly mattered to me, sad to say. I

> *Cleverness and persuasiveness are actually praised as an achievement as we grow up, as long as there is evidence of material or personal success.*

realized years later that good salesmanship was not necessarily a virtue. Getting that sale was the driving force of every aspiring salesman, and we were praised for it. My sales manager was respected and admired in his field, and pressured all of us to go for the maximum sale possible. I would bring him contract after contract and he would tell me I needed more to even be average, while unbeknownst to me I was breaking national sales records.

I often wondered, years later, how many of my low-income customers were able to make their payments, and how many of them had purchased the products because of all the clever angles I had learned to get people to buy what I was selling. They wanted what I was selling because I convinced them the products I was selling would make them happy, with compelling, illustrated material furnished by the company to back it up.

Persuasiveness is considered an extremely marketable skill. The better you become at it, the more people will admire you. The more evidence of success, the more someone is praised and exalted. We promote these "successful people," and seminars and workshops on persuasiveness and persistence in business proliferate around the country. We elect the most persuasive and convincing candidates to political office, where such skills are even more finely honed with little regard for the character, motives or underlying intentions of the great persuaders they become.

I'm not casting aspersions at politicians. Whether their actions come from truth or political maneuvering, they're a more visible and well-known example of what people learn to do to get ahead. All too often they cross a line, and then another and another. But something is lost in the process. What is lost when truth is compromised is core integrity – the one thing that gives value and purpose to everything we should do as individuals, as communities and ultimately as a truly civilized society. I believe if Merlin were real and alive today, he would walk away and not even bother to tell us how far we have strayed and how much we have lost that is of real value in life. Something is steadily dying in our society – something that's required for any moral society to sustain itself through the challenges that face each generation.

The moral fabric of our country – the bedrock upon which everything is based – is eroding at a rate that is mind-numbing. Few can even recognize truth at this point such that we have no idea how to course-correct to bring ourselves back on track. It's so difficult to believe people when they tell you certain things, especially things that make a difference in your life. Does a real estate agent reveal all the imperfections of a home you're considering buying? Not likely. They're just "imperfections," after all. What about harried sales managers with quotas to meet and bottom lines to constantly improve? His or her job and income depend upon meeting those quotas and bottom lines, and many of them will do what it takes to meet them.

How many law enforcement scandals have we experienced, Presidents impeached, and priests, Boy Scout leaders, movie producers and stars and schoolteachers convicted for moral deviance? Who tells the truth, and who can you believe? More importantly, how has this maddening cycle affected you? If an error in a financial transaction is made in your favor, do you give it back? Are you willing to tell the truth about something even if it makes you look bad? Do you shade the truth a little if it gives you an advantage over someone? What if you're confronted about something you said or did…do you avoid the repercussions by denying it or discounting it?

You might be quick to say yes to these questions because they seem obvious, but think again. Observe yourself for the next few weeks and see how you do. I do it all the time, and even as self-conscious as I am about it, I'm mystified by how easily my inner-knave will bend the truth or justify even the tiniest misstep. If you can still say yes to those questions as you go through your daily routines, you're way ahead of most people. It's not as easy as it seems. Truth is nuanced and often has many layers of interpretation and rationalization.

Thankfully, I've met a number of people who are truthful in all of their dealings. Whenever I do, I feel an instant friendship and trust in the first moments I meet them. That's because there's integrity with no extra energy or "fluff" around it. A famous broadcast journalist of the last century, Walter Cronkite, was a natural truth-teller when he anchored the evening news for many years. He was considered by most people in those days to be "the most honest man in America." He was revered by all who listened to him.

> *Where there is true integrity, there is no extra energy or "fluff" involved. It just flows naturally, and you can feel it.*

Trust between people is an inner knowing. We're born with it as part of our internal guidance system. It's a natural, innate sense before it becomes diluted and distorted as we grow up. Gradually, when we've been lied to enough times, we lose our ability to access it. We stop trusting what we feel inside.

One person's truth can be quite different from another. Many diverse truths exist between different cultures and religions. But truth doesn't change just because it wears different religious or cultural clothing, or is written in religious or spiritual books. Truths between people are built from a common respect for one another's existence, and are demonstrated by our words and actions.

Even hardened inmates know when they're lying or telling the truth. Our politicians should, and we should hold them accountable for what they say and promise. To not stand up and point out inaccuracies or lies is to become an accomplice to them. Standing up for the truth often comes with risk when it runs against the grain of accepted mistruths, and that takes courage.

If you're already living a totally honest, truthful life in every respect, then keep on. You're an example for others. But if you cut corners from time to time to save a few dollars, or time or ego, you might want to slow down and consider some healthy alternatives... like truth. What's really going on with you? Simple laziness or habit patterns? Whatever you want to change about yourself can be changed. Watch and listen. When you notice yourself shading the truth, cutting corners, or dancing around a delicate subject, tell the truth. Be authentic and genuine. Be real. Don't judge yourself or make excuses. Sometimes you don't even have to do anything. Just noticing the pattern often enough will subconsciously begin the change. It takes very little effort to see where you might be stuck, but it does require some effort to change the patterns and create new, more meaningful habits.

Regardless of the outcome, that simple act of courage will be a significant step toward personal freedom. Even if the situation blows up and you lose a friend, or money, or worse, the self-respect and empowerment you will gain by changing the patterns of your thinking and behavior will be worth the cost. You will reach some illuminating moments and epiphanies along the way. If you trip up or stumble, that's okay. The goal isn't perfection. The goal is authenticity. Shake it off and keep moving forward.

Asking for honest feedback from close friends and family can be helpful. It can inspire their own introspection, but use discretion and discernment. As you are more real with yourself and others, the example you'll set will either cause others to trust you, or not to trust you because they may be jaded by past behavior and will question your motives. Be ready for either reaction, but remain steadfast about making the changes you wish and don't allow others' opinions and projections to sway or deter you.

There is a place for honesty and truth at all levels of government, commerce, and religion…and in our individual lives. It should be at the very top of our priorities, but it has to start at the individual level or it will never get to the higher levels. If enough of us are willing to tell and live the truth in our everyday lives and relationships, the ripple effect would change everything we know about our world.

It doesn't matter whether you change the world or not. What matters is that you're willing to change *your world* and your perspective in an effort to improve yourself, one day at a time. When there is truth in your relationships and truth in how you see yourself, there's more time available to feel true joy in your life. Without wasting energy by lying and covering up those lies, you're allowing more positive energy to flow more naturally into your life. We still have to be adults, parents, and whatever roles we've created to play out in our lives, but we'll have more enjoyment in *being* those things.

It gives new meaning and value to the adage, *What goes around, comes around.*

CHAPTER SEVEN

Trust

I was born into a middle-class American family, the son of a career military officer, and raised during the "Baby-Boomer" era when the American Dream was off to a robust start. It was a time of war heroes, movie stars, cheap gasoline, and plenty of jobs and opportunities for everyone. Or so it seemed. Terms like love, honor and trust were foregone conclusions.

America had become the world's protectors, so everything we did seemed right and honorable. We were the victors of a long and brutal world war, and had sacrificed fathers, brothers, sons and even sisters and daughters so that everyone everywhere would be free to pursue their dreams. Because we were moral, ethical and stronger than other nations, everything we did was assumed by us to be good. Who could know more about virtues like honor, respect and trust than we did? After all, we had lost countless lives fighting foreign wars presumably to secure and uphold those values.

But somewhere along the way, things went wrong. Whether you were born into a middle-class or lower-income family, a common delusion developed that if one's intentions were good and the image they maintained was proper, everything would work out for the best.

That attitude was fueled by the successful outcome of a recent global war, and was carried out as a central theme over the next two decades by a plethora of media across America. It was an indelible part of an economic boom that gave resurgent life to the long-buried notion that "might makes right"…more acceptable now as long as "might" came cloaked in red, white and blue.

If you were lucky, you were born to parents who loved you regardless of their social status. The notion that anyone and everyone who worked hard enough could become anything they wanted became America's motto. Mistakes and problems you had along the way were as easily resolved as they were in TV shows like *Father Knows Best, Lassie, Bonanza*, and others popular during the 1960's. You knew you had value, even if you didn't have a clue who you were, or where you stood in the social and cultural pecking order of life. If things didn't quite make sense, you'd figure it out in college – if you were lucky enough to go to college – or else on a construction site or in one of the many sports arenas and playing fields across America. Until that point, you would do whatever it took to pursue your dreams, even if it were only maintaining a well-practiced image until you achieved them.

If you weren't so lucky, you found out pretty early-on that love, honor, and trust were just words. They sounded good, but had no real substance or permanence while you were struggling to figure out how money and power worked when you didn't have any. You didn't feel valued, so you had no point of reference from which to draw on things like honor and trust. Until you found out how things really worked, you acted as if you knew. You would "fake it until you make it," as the common saying went, and as a result you learned the importance of a good image by seeing how much others seemed willing to sacrifice in order to keep theirs intact.

Wherever you were on the spectrum of life, the need to *appear* trustworthy gradually replaced the need to actually *be* trustworthy. The economy continued to climb, jobs were plentiful, and everything seemed to be working well. There was no need to rock the boat as long as the boat seemed headed in the right direction.

No matter who we were, however, the mistruths, vanities, and outright lies caused us to lose our trust in the system, authority figures, and gradually each other. Many of us Baby-Boomers became flower children and dropped out of schools and workplaces to find ourselves. We didn't trust anyone over thirty, or who wore a tie, a uniform, a badge, or an apron. What has resulted is a nation of people so caught up in maintaining images that truth and authenticity have become merely abstract words.

The good news in all of what has taken place in the past two decades may be that many of us are waking up to the reality and power of personal choice. Just reading this book is a step in a meaningful direction because if you sense that even some of this material might be of value to you, then you can accept that trust, like gratitude, is an attitude over which you have complete control. Once you understand what trust actually is, how it works and why it's so important, you will understand how the other attributes in this book are related. Trust, like gratitude, is a matter of personal and collective choice. If we don't exercise conscious choice, we default to what we have subconsciously learned, *even if it's wrong*. If we live our lives hiding behind masks that we think others need to see, and settling for less than what we really want, we tend to forget that they're only masks, and we become them.

Speaking of masks, I once met Clayton Moore, the original "Lone Ranger" of the 1950's television series. He was alone in a coffee shop in a hotel in San Antonio where I had an important meeting later that morning. The waitress excitedly pointed him out to me, and I was bewildered. This was no 6'2" pearl-handled, six-gun-toting masked man who rode the Wild West on his white stallion, saving people from bad guys. This was a shriveled-up old man, hunched over his table with a pair of over-sized, wrap-around sunglasses on his face. No way this man could be the nemesis of outlaws of the Old West. Momentarily forgetting about my impending meeting with some real-life bad guys upstairs, I approached him. Just as I neared his table, he looked up and noticeably tensed up.

"Excuse me, Sir," I spoke hesitantly.

"Yes, I'm Clayton Moore, if that's what you want to know," he cut me off, obviously irritated. "You looking for an autograph?" He was clearly not a man content with his life.

"No, Sir…not that I wouldn't accept one, but I just had to find out…"

"Well, now you know. I really am the Lone Ranger…or *was* once." His emphasis on "was" fell heavily on my heart. This was my boyhood hero, if this was true. "I'm here for a fund-raiser," he continued, "and I have to wear these damn sunglasses because the studio I worked for filed a lawsuit to prevent me from wearing the mask."

"What?" I asked. "How could that be? It's just a mask. Anyone can wear a mask."

"Not that one…believe me. It was a long and bitter fight. They won, so I have to wear these."

We talked for a little longer, and I wished him well. I had business upstairs, but I never forgot the bitterness I felt in this aging icon from my boyhood days. That mask and his blue, full-length, cowboy outfit, black leather boots, and gun belt with real silver bullets gave him his power and persona for decades.

The meeting I had was with the head of an organization that had hired me to set up an air freight business for their extensive drug smuggling business, and I had reached a point where I knew I was in deep trouble if I stayed with them. Fortunately, I had developed a good rapport with the older man who ran the business. He and I had walked together on remote, Caribbean beaches and told each other stories of our fathers and our boyhood dreams. He appreciated my honesty and openness, but his younger brother, a typical Mafioso-type, did not. He was enraged that I might suggest quitting, and let me know in no uncertain way. The Old Man shushed him, shook my hand warmly and assured me that I was welcome to come back anytime and work for them.

That was only slightly reassuring to me as I made my way from their suite to the nearest elevator wondering when the guns with the silencers might put an end to my cavalier story. Nervously, I waited for the elevator door to open. When it did, I nearly went weak in the knees.

Front and center with a number of awe-struck people huddled in the back stood the Lone Ranger himself – tall and imposing in his full regalia – blue cowboy outfit, black cowboy boots and gun belt, and those silly, wraparound sunglasses on his face. I never felt so relieved in my life. Somehow, at the scariest moment of my life, I had managed to pull my boyhood hero out of my past as if to rescue me in a modern-day hotel in San Antonio. I took a deep breath of relief, stepped onboard and moved gingerly into position right behind him. My disbelieving eyes couldn't help but notice only four of his famous silver bullets still in his gun belt, attesting to the probability that his studio wouldn't let him have any more of them, either.

We got to the parking garage level and everyone exited, including the cowboy hero looking like a Hollywood prop. I walked as closely behind him as I could without looking too obvious, and when I got to my car he kept on walking. Part of me wanted to follow him to see if he got on his horse and rode off, or what kind of vehicle someone like him could possibly drive without looking absurd. But the irony of his presence in my life at that very point was not lost on me, nor is it now as I write this chapter and consider the immense value we unwittingly place on the masks we wear and the images we show to the world.

That happened in early 1980. It was the beginning of the "Me First" decade, characterized by the fast and furious or the slick and pretty. Image was all that really mattered back then, regardless of the rhetoric spewing out from podiums and pulpits. It was the time of the rise and fall of religious icons such as televangelist Jimmy Swaggart, famous for his 10,000+ fanatical audiences; Tammy Faye and Jim Baker and their Bible-themed amusement park; and a seemingly endless stream of shady evangelists, corrupt politicians, and corporate connivers that built and destroyed some of the biggest corporations in history over the next two decades. It also saw a Chief of Naval Operations – the third-highest-ranking admiral in the U.S. Navy – take his own life over the discovery that he had accepted an unearned medal in his earlier years. He had many distinguished and well-deserved medals, yet he ended his career and his life over accepting one that wasn't even combat-related. If there was any trust for authority left in my troubled young mind by that time, it was gone for good as far as I was concerned.

It didn't matter, though. By that time I was dealing with a legal mess of my own, and trust had become just another myth to me, like the Lone Ranger, Superman, and dozens of real-life celebrities. One of them was George Reeves, who played the original Superman at about the same time as the Lone Ranger. He committed suicide, which was super-odd, and so did Bob Crane, the mischievous colonel of *Hogan's Heroes*. Then the "King of Rock & Roll," Elvis Presley, overdosed on pills and booze, and so did everyone's favorite blonde at the time, Marilyn Monroe, who by that time most everyone knew, or strongly suspected, had been the mistress of our assassinated President, JFK. My own father took his life when I was barely sixteen, and much later, my eldest sister.

> *But the upside of all this – if there is one – is that this all came about because of societal beliefs we had cultivated over generations. As with any beliefs, however, they can be changed.*

Our heroes and heroines, celebrities, authority figures and members of my own family were either dying like flies, or were in and out of rehab centers, divorce courts, or impeachment proceedings.

But the upside of all this – if there is one – is that this all came about because of societal beliefs we had cultivated over generations. As with any beliefs, however, they can be changed. In order for them to change on a scale that could hope to balance those kinds of odds, they have to change on an individual level first…and in no small way. We have to take stock of where we're at now as individuals, and how we do even the simplest things honorably.

Consider your basic interactions with others, and really make an effort with this because it will change your life for the better if you do. Do you keep your agreements with everyone? Are you on time with appointments…even small things like meeting a friend for coffee or lunch? Do you say one thing and then do something else? Are you constantly running late, making excuses or forgetting things you said you would do?

Not only do such things send a message of disrespect that tells others not to trust you (even if they love you), but each incident deepens a belief and a pattern in your own mind that you are not trustworthy. It has been clinically proven that every time you break a promise or fail to keep simple agreements with others, your mind records the event and keeps track of the number of times you do it. No matter how well you might justify the reasons, your mind knows that you've been untrustworthy…repeatedly. In order to compensate for that weakness, most people overcompensate with increasing amounts of bravado, patronizing behavior, or arrogance or indifference. But your mind doesn't forget. We get so caught up in these patterns that we lose track of how to be our authentic selves. When we do get some counseling, or good advice, and want to change the behavior, it's tough because our mind has ample proof that we're unreliable and untrustworthy. That's why it takes time, and a lot of effort to break the pattern.

Then there's all that conditioning from childhood. We think we are too small, too insignificant to make a difference, but nothing could be farther from the truth. Everything that exists in any society's development is a collective result of individual thinking and behaving. It might be helpful to consider such things as how you feel when someone makes a commitment to you that you know is likely to go unfulfilled, and how you feel when you tell someone you intend to meet them at some point when you know that it's not likely to happen. How many times have you told someone you want to get together someday, and seldom do?

On the positive side, consider how you felt when someone actually kept their word with you, or did something surprisingly attentive and respectful of you…even something as simple as remembered your birthday and took the time to acknowledge it. Things like that make both people feel good inside, knowing that you matter to each other. You can do that with anyone, even if it just a simple greeting to show that they matter.

Work on the little things you can easily do each day. This takes a disciplined mind, but that will come with practice if you're serious about positive change in your life. It takes a lot of positive reinforcement of the little things before the bigger things begin to change. Then apply this to larger changes. Done often enough with the small things, your mind will shift into thought patterns that you can be trusted to keep your word, and it will gradually make sure that you do. That's how to change habit patterns. People who are serious about personal growth and development spend thousands of dollars for retreats and extended seminars and personal growth training to change the kind of habit patterns to which I'm referring. These are changes you can do on your own, for *free*.

Think of trust like a bank account. Each agreement kept is like a deposit, while each agreement or promise missed is a withdrawal. If the latter outnumbers the former, you need to work harder to balance your trust account until there is a positive balance. Then the work becomes far easier because establishing trust in all your relationships and interactions has become normal for you.

A lot of people who spend a lot of time and money on self-help seminars revert back to old patterns of behavior at some point. Why? Sometimes new patterns are too rigid, with so much structure that they feel unnatural and too formidable to uphold. And that's okay. The lessons learned and insights gained are still part of your memory and psyche. There are many stories about people who did well for a while, fell away from that type of thinking, and then years later suddenly remembered some of the positive changes they felt in the beginning, and got back into it on their own. Positive change comes when it comes. Give yourself time to feel what's right for you. Like a lot of weight loss diets, changes will come far more effectively and will be more lasting and meaningful if you make them because you really want to rather than to force yourself.

You may be a good mother or father, a good teacher or whatever profession you have chosen. If you long to tap into your deeper purpose and achieve something greater, something beyond the regular workaday world in which you now live, you need to trust in a deeper, inner process that may be stirring in you to be recognized and cultivated.

During that dark time in my past, I made a frantic phone call to a mentor of mine. I was calling him *collect,* from jail, and told him that things looked pretty dismal.

"How exciting!" he said to me, as if I had just told him I was going for a ride on the space shuttle. I stood bewildered for a moment looking at the phone, not believing what I was hearing from this man of deep wisdom while all around me were muscle-bound, tattooed gladiator types glaring at me like I was fresh meat. But knowing him as well as I did, I instinctively knew what he meant and it forced a chuckle in spite of my circumstances.

> *This is your stage, your show. There's something to be learned from this, or you wouldn't have created it. Trust the process.*

After a moment or two, he went on. "Don't get caught up in the images," he said. "You created this for a reason that's deeper than what seems obvious. You'll be okay. This is your stage…your show. There's something to be learned from this, or you wouldn't have created it. Just trust the process."

The same is true for you, whatever the circumstances of your own life. I've met people who have endured far more challenging situations than mine, and in every case where they accepted responsibility for having put forces in motion that resulted in each situation, their outlook and attitude became powerful examples of drawing strength from adversity, and created inspiring lifestyles. Many of them are now doing prison reform work, teaching school, or working on projects for the homeless or women's shelters. They're everyday heroes, as far as I'm concerned, and are being increasingly recognized as role models they never intended to be. I'm one of them.

> *It doesn't matter what happens to you. It only matters what you do with what happens to you.*

It doesn't matter what happens to you, I often say to people facing personal challenges and difficulties. It only matters *what you do with what happens to you.*

It doesn't matter who you are, where you come from or how much education or money you have. If you believe that on some level you created every experience in your life as something from which to learn, you will achieve success and happiness. That doesn't mean that there won't be heartache, sadness or disappointment along the way. But it does mean that even the darkest storm clouds are only temporary. They can wreak havoc in your life for a while, but they will pass. The less you look at yourself and others as victims, and instead as co-creators of life's many mysteries, the more you can understand why things are the way they are. Using positive thoughts and the other principles and core values in this book, you can turn these challenges into better, more meaningful realities. That's why they exist…to give us something to do besides simply making it from the cradle to the grave in one piece.

You're in charge of your life no matter what the outward circumstances may be. Big Jim came to realize that he was ultimately the one in charge – at least of his *mind,* if not his physical location – until he gained his release. He gave full credit to God for the grace that came to him in that putrid hell-hole where he was locked up for eighteen months with the door welded shut, but he discovered also that he was the one who had the self-determination and personal strength not to give up and to trust that he was being led somewhere meaningful.

"If you can step back far enough in your mind," said my mentor, "you can see the forces at play, balancing things out no matter how unfair they might appear." He was right. No matter what I look at in my life, I can always "step back" and see how and why I marshaled the forces I did in each process. I haven't mastered the art quite yet, but I'm getting better at it. Hopefully, we never stop learning. I believe there is a divine, creative force behind everything. It's up to each of us to learn from our experiences, and then act accordingly. It requires trust on such a deep level that we are unshakeable on our journey Homeward – whatever form you believe that to be.

With steadfast right attitude, which includes trust at its core, you have total control over your future and your destiny. There is always hope, and, with enough time, trust and practice, that hope is turned into reality. That goes along with courage enough to see it through until the purpose for which you came here is clear to you. With that, you can make a real difference in your life, and in the world. You can even bank on it because your "accounts" will be balanced and in the black.

"Integrity, the choice between what's convenient and what's right."

— Tony Dungy

CHAPTER EIGHT
Integrity

Integrity is one of those words like love, honor and trust that is so common in our everyday language that people think they know what each one means. But in fact, integrity means something quite different to different people, depending upon cultural differences, attitudes, education and individual usage. One might think someone has integrity because he or she says the right things or appears to have the right look or feel, but if we look more deeply and observe that person under varying conditions of stress, worry or duress, we might find that integrity is not the word that would describe them best.

For many of us, integrity tends to be a term of convenience because, depending upon how it's used, it can sound very convincing if it's said often enough about someone, or by people of influence and authority. But that doesn't necessarily make that person someone of integrity. Sadly, it's often quite the contrary, especially if it's used too often or with too much effort to persuade.

Integrity is something that just *is*. A person either has integrity, or doesn't. It's not something you do halfway, or use to suit your own purposes and needs, no matter how well-intentioned you might be. Rather, it's a state of being. You can't *intend* to have integrity. You can make mistakes and still have integrity if you are willing to be honest about them and make the effort to correct them. But you can't have integrity by merely intending to have it. It's like saying to someone when you've messed something up, "…but I really *meant* well." Integrity would be taking immediate responsibility for the deed that was done, apologizing and taking steps to repair or correct the problem that arose from the action.

> *Integrity is not something you do halfway, or use to suit your own purposes and needs. Rather, it's a state of being.*

Integrity doesn't mean perfection, but rather a person of integrity acknowledges his or her mistakes, accepts them as part of being human, and moves on with courage and willingness to be transparent and genuine. A person of integrity can be counted on to tell the truth no matter what, and is someone others feel instantly comfortable around because nothing feels hidden, deceptive, or manipulative.

Unfortunately, people who know how to manipulate others can use the appearance of integrity to get their way which, sadly, characterizes much of our political system and our corporate world. What makes it so insidious, however, is the degree to which that attitude permeates everything to the extent that many people who use the guise of integrity to succeed, do so without even realizing how they compromise themselves. The whole concept of integrity, like honor and love, has become so arbitrary and conditional that few people even know what it is. They talk about it as if they do, and may even feel they are a person of integrity if they're seeking a leadership position or promoting the merits of a business, but neither situation necessarily or automatically makes one a person of integrity.

Beyond The Chaos — Integrity

I believe most everyone wants to be thought of as having integrity, but one need only look around at how we are entertained, advertised to and conditioned by virtually all walks of business, politics, religion and even education to get a sense of how far we've gotten off-track. I read somewhere that our children see over 12,000 killings on television during their upbringing, and all the violence, mayhem, and deception that goes with that, all for the sake of advertisers and videogame makers to make money. I'm all for free enterprise and *responsible* capitalism, so making money is fine – but a society that allows that sort of business to be promoted to its youth without responsible regulation and monitoring is a society virtually devoid of integrity on a collective and individual level. It damages the psyche of our youth to think that killing of anything so randomly and wantonly is an acceptable and normal thing to do. It's no wonder there has been such an increase in random mass shootings.

> "Live so that when your children think of fairness, caring and integrity, they think of you."
> – H. Jackson Brown, Jr.

The results of this lack of integrity on so many levels are clearly evidenced by the many failures and upheavals we have experienced in recent decades with presidents impeached, political and religious leaders jailed, and major corporations collapsed under the greed and avarice of leaders we thought had integrity or were led to believe they did. The prevalence of drugs and alcohol abuse further shows our lack of integrity as people who will do anything to avoid taking responsibility for the chaos and mayhem that exists in the world today.

How do we know what integrity really is when our leaders

apparently don't, or don't care to? Where did we get off the track? What role models do we have to show us how to live and be in a state of integrity? Where do we start, and how do we get others to act out of integrity? How can one individual make a difference when it's all so distorted and out of balance?

Once again, integrity is a state of mind, which, if desired strongly by enough people and pursued with determination, honesty and consistency, becomes a state of *being.* It's not something someone does, or pretends to be, but rather who someone *is.* That doesn't mean being flawless. Rather, it means being in a state of truth and transparency about who you are, *flaws included,* and how openly you communicate with others. A person of integrity doesn't tell others he or she has integrity, nor do they even imply it. It's in their manner, and how they live each day. Once structured and set deeply enough, it becomes a constant in one's outward behavior because it's an inward habit and pattern. It's unquestioned by others because they can feel it.

Martin Luther King had integrity, without a doubt. So did Mother Theresa. Did they make mistakes? Yes, of course. I'm sure at times they erred as much as any of us. They were human. They readily admitted they weren't always right or perfect. But they didn't let personal needs or desires distract them, or get in the way of finding their own truth and striving to perfect themselves. They didn't posture or use pretense to accomplish their objectives. Gandhi, in his younger years, was temperamental and somewhat arrogant at times. But he had integrity enough to recognize his weaknesses and the desire to work through them to become a more effective change-maker. Humility became his greatest strength, ultimately, along with courage to stay that way in the face of powerful forces of resistance and oppression.

As Lincoln said, "You can fool some of the people all the time, and all of the people some of the time. But you can't fool all the people all the time." I believe that he was essentially talking about integrity. You can't impact or inspire people at the level that he, or Gandhi, Martin Luther King or Mother Theresa did without integrity. Integrity is, above all, consistent.

You might think, "I'm no Mother Theresa or Gandhi. I have no interest or desire to do what they did." That's understandable and reasonable, but not fair to the people you can impact positively, which includes your*self*. The great visionaries I've mentioned each found their calling as they were doing other more normal things, and as they aligned themselves with a higher purpose their vision and impact grew. They didn't start out as giants. Very few of the ones I've read about had any notion when they started about the future impact they would have on masses of humanity, and on history.

> *A person of integrity doesn't tell others he or she has integrity, nor do they even imply it. It's in their manner, and how they live each day.*

Unfortunately, people like that only come along every few decades. When they do, we put them on pedestals or make saints out of them, or we fear them and persecute them. Later, after they've gone, we realize the good they did and we consider them "holy," or "divinely guided." We separate them in our minds from us as the human beings they were, and we forget they were just like us at one point in their lives. We make ourselves smaller in the process, and allow ourselves to think we can't be as strong, clear or powerful.

But we can. We don't have to give inspired speeches to throngs of devoted admirers, or live austere lives, or run for political office, but we can live heroically and powerfully by striving to achieve a state of real integrity in our everyday lives. That doesn't require anything but personal courage and a willingness to be honest. Integrity for most people takes a lot of courage because it runs against the grain, so to speak, of what is common or popular. It also takes a willingness to stand for your beliefs, if you even know what they are. That's another subject, but in the meantime you can start with always telling the truth about everything – not just the things you choose to be truthful about and being sloppy with the less important things.

Integrity is a constant striving for clarity and truth in simple, everyday living. It's a rare thing to encounter these days, so it may be hard to spot or recognize, and even harder to cultivate in ourselves with the twisted and convoluted upbringing many of us have had. But you can always tell someone's lack of integrity by the degree to which they seem to need to reinforce their image or acceptability in the minds of others.

"Let me be honest with you," is an all too common expression in general conversation. Think about that. Why would someone say that unless they haven't been honest with you up to that point? A person of integrity wouldn't even think that, let alone say it. The statement, "I am a person of integrity," or anything like that, is a sort of oxymoron. Integrity doesn't need to announce or identify itself, and it can't be wished for or intended. It either is, or it isn't.

Do you tell the truth about everything? That question was posed in a previous chapter, and it's a question that you want to ask yourself on a daily basis. We've learned from an early age to say what we think needs to be said in order to appease others as we make our way through life. We do it so quickly and automatically that even as the words come out of our mouths, our minds are busily concocting justifications for what we're saying. We get lost in a charade of words and rationalizations made worse because success in our society is determined by how well one plays the game.

Don't you tire of that game? Don't you long for people to speak the truth and be genuine, honest, and reliable? Wouldn't you prefer to set an example for our nation's children so they will know what integrity is, and become the noble leaders we seek so we won't have to wait a few decades for another Gandhi or Martin Luther King to surface? If we don't live that way ourselves, what will be the incentive for our children to do so, and what are we leaving behind for them? We've created very murky waters of immorality, deception, and uncertainty for them to deal with, and we need to clean that up before we pass on.

> *Integrity doesn't need to announce or identify itself, and it can't be wished for or intended. It either is or it isn't.*

How do we do that? We start each day with a firm resolve to live honorably and to observe ourselves more objectively. We watch more closely and listen more carefully – first to ourselves and then to others as we engage them. Read that line again, and think about it for a moment. Don't let these be just words on paper. *Do what they say, and practice it. You'll change your life for the better.* Practice observing yourself without self-criticism, judgment or blame. Watch what you say, think and do, and what others say and do with one another. And then, before you go to sleep at night, review the day as best you can, and think about how it went and what you could have done better…again, without judging or condemning yourself. Integrity isn't an end game. It's an ongoing process of being determined to clean up your life and be of good moral character, reliable and trustworthy. It takes time to cultivate that, considering how most of us have been raised.

As you begin to do that, you will make imperceptible changes in your behavior that will reshape and redefine who you are and how you think as you continue to build on it. The reason for that is that in our hearts, most of us know what's right and what isn't. Unless we're completely asleep or numbed by alcohol, drugs, or other addictive behavior, we know when we're covering something up, cutting corners, or generally being sloppy with our manners or our words. We know when we're not telling the truth. We're creatures of habit. Changing habits isn't easy because those habits are so ingrained in us. We *can* change them, however, and as we do, we won't feel the need to say to someone else, "Let me be honest with you." Being honest will come naturally and effortlessly.

One of the most amazing things about self-reflection is how simple it is once you start. If you are willing to be honest with yourself, and then outwardly with others, your life will change…very slightly at first, perhaps, but much more notably as you dig deeper and act more boldly with the revelations and discoveries that come to you. If you do everything honestly and impeccably, even when no one is watching you, then you are in a state of integrity. Your actions and your attitude, even your very presence, will say that about you, and with increasing impact because you will be *living* it rather than talking about it.

I lived near the Canadian border for a while, and once had lunch with a new Canadian friend. In a short time, we were deep in discussion about drug use and the political scene in both countries, terrorism around the world and how pervasive fear is in the hearts and minds of people everywhere.

As we talked, I felt a sense of helplessness and resignation building in both of us, and then I remembered some of what I've come to learn about integrity and the other principles and values I'm writing about now. I began to talk with him

> *If you do everything honestly and impeccably, even when no one is watching you, then you are in a state of integrity.*

about those principles, and how we can change things just by embracing them, and then incorporating them into our thinking and behavior. I hesitated at first, not wanting to seem naïve or impractical, or "preachy," but then pressed on with just a few simple comments about how important it is that we be willing to start first with ourselves and be willing to believe that small actions might make a difference.

As I talked, I felt my confidence building and noticed that he was paying attention. Where before I might have felt apologetic or dismissive of what may have seemed abstract or unimportant subjects, I pressed on with how the "ripple effect" could be powerful, but that in order to be so, it had to come from deep, inner conviction and knowing in each of us.

He was noticeably interested in what I had to say, and then began to talk along the same lines. He had the same concerns that I did for his nearly grown-up son as I have for my children, and for their children. Then we realized we could make a difference at least in those lives, and in the lives of our co-workers, friends, and other family members just by setting an example. Such small changes can make huge differences if people we talk to in turn believe that they, too, can make a difference.

What does that really mean, anyway…"making a difference?" We hear it all the time, to the point where many of us just get numb to the words. It's too big, too abstract or too nebulous. Noble as those words may seem, we need to shift our focus to something measurable and real – something we can see and feel more perceptively, such as I noticed with my Canadian friend. My words impacted him, and gave him reason to pause and think a bit more deeply about what we were saying. We had just been to a movie and were enjoying some reflective thoughts over the ideals and principles portrayed in the film, but instead of getting into more banal "guy talk," we talked about what's really important. We were even sitting in a sports bar, but didn't pay attention to the different "guy" things flashing on all the screens.

It mattered to us what we were saying to each other because we had for the moment chosen to take the time to not only talk, but to *listen* with interest to one another, and it made a difference in how we perceived one another and spoke with each other. That's been happening to me with increasing frequency. I think most everyone, except fanatics, wants to know how to get ourselves out of the madness going on in the world.

It has nothing to do with the economic or political unrest in the world. Our global problems are only outward symptoms of something much more fundamental in each of us. Rather, it is the need we have to be respected and valued, as I wrote earlier. In order to have value, we need to come from a place of clarity and integrity *within ourselves*. That can be just as valid for a poppy farmer in Afghanistan or an inmate in a prison as it should be for someone running for political office…or a banker, doctor, teacher, parent or young adults trying to navigate their way through what's going on in the world.

There was a man in the community where I spent much of the past twenty-five years who, until his death many years ago, did more to instill in me some of the values of which I now write than anyone who ever preached to me. He was a pilot, and owned the only air charter business in our remote community. He was humble, respectful of everyone, and never was heard to say a bad thing about anyone, despite a bitter and almost hateful wife. Perhaps it was his Baptist upbringing, or the minister he had been in his earlier years, but he never "preached" to me. He just lived the principles I have been writing about.

He set an example by his everyday actions, words, and thoughts. He clearly was a man of integrity, and it showed in the humble, gentle, and respectful way he treated everyone. Because of the impact he had on me, I still remember him and the lessons learned just from being around him as if it were only a few years ago. You never know what kind of impact you can have on others. In the movie, *Mr. Holland's Opus,* Richard Dreyfuss plays the part of a musician just out of college pursuing his dream to become a composer and write his own opus. He takes a part-time job as a high school music teacher, and decades later he's still teaching music in the same high school. He's now in his sixties and retiring. As his final days wind down, he reflects on his life and begins to feel a sense of loss that he never achieved his dream. I don't want to spoil the movie for you if you've never seen it, so I won't tell you what happens, but it's worth watching even if you've seen it before. It's a beautiful, heartwarming example of the "ripple effect," which I've mentioned before.

    Every once in a while, someone comes up and tells me what a big difference I've made in their lives, and I'm always surprised when they do. Then I remember a line from the movie, *Pretty Woman,* when the two lead characters are comparing notes on how each of them is perceived by others. One comes from opulence and the other from poverty and struggle, but both agree it's easier to believe the bad things that are said about them. That may have been true for me in the past, and may be true for you. But it doesn't have to be that way.

    Only you can change that, and you do it by watching your everyday choices of attitude and outlook. As you do, you will notice changes taking place both inside and out. To the degree that you are willing to be objective and honest with yourself and others, your life will change, and you *will* "make a difference" in the world and in the lives of those with whom you connect and interact. As you do, and others do so as well, the problems of the world won't seem so chaotic, heartless, or mean-spirited. Gradually, at first, then increasingly as more and more people catch on, we will see the day when respect, honor, and real integrity characterize what people think, say and do –

and we will see value, purpose and direction restored in our lives, and in the lives of others.

As the worn out saying goes, "It all starts with you." But to make it less worn-out and more of a reality in the world, you have to put it into daily practice. Make it a part of everything you do, and before long it will become a habit…one that will keep a smile on your face until that day when you pass your torch along to future generations.

"Life is no brief candle to me. It is a sort of splendid torch, which I've got hold of for a brief moment. I want to make it burn as brightly as possible before handing it on to future generations."

– George Bernard Shaw

*"Be kind.
For everyone you meet
is fighting a battle
you know nothing about."*

— Ian MacClaran

CHAPTER
NINE

The Injunctions

There are many impediments to our growth and success in life, but there are three in particular that affect us more than most because we don't even know they exist. They are attitudes and beliefs we acquire from childhood that to a somewhat harmful extent we learn to embrace and accept as perfectly normal ways of thinking. We know about the limiting beliefs many of us are taught, such as "we're not good enough," and "there's not enough," and "starving children in China," but these are more subtly ingrained in us than that. Not knowing about them and how they influence us can impede our progress in life no matter how well we do in school, sports, entertainment, or any other pursuits. Knowing how to release ourselves from their influence can be among the most liberating experiences of our growth and awareness.

In one of the human growth and awareness seminars I attended, the facilitator spoke of these impediments to our growth and self-understanding, and developed some guidelines for how to overcome them. He called them "Injunctions" – guidelines to help overcome limitations that keep us unknowingly stuck in old behaviors.

The First Injunction is Not to Judge. This does not mean you can't make judgments, nor am I referring to the kind of judgment that is needed in a courtroom, in traffic or on an athletic field. Rather, it has to do with how we place a value on each other before we've had an opportunity to get to know one another. Our first impressions of each other set the tone for whether we are going to engage with each other or not, and on what basis. Subconscious thoughts such as "this person is better than me," or "this person is lesser than me," form in our minds almost immediately upon encountering people we don't know.

Do you ever catch yourself doing that? It's almost automatic for many people, and has its roots in the need to use caution in encountering anything and anyone who might be harmful to us. It's important to use common sense and intuition when encountering people we don't know, which is not an easy thing to do in today's world of pandemics, political strife, disinformation and fast-paced living. A judgment about someone is not necessarily bad, since we need to know how safe, reliable, or decent someone is…or isn't. What I'm talking about is letting our perception of someone's worth cloud our sense of who they really are or how accurate or inaccurate our opinion of them might be. Our pre-conceived notions about them can prevent us from getting to know someone with whom we might otherwise have a good friendship and a valuable and rewarding experience.

When you place a value on a person, you separate yourself from them with a distance in direct proportion to your perception of them as being of greater or lesser value than you. In the process, you fail to engage that person on a more equal or open basis, and you lose the opportunity to discover anything about them or gain something in the process. To be more objective, when our opinion of someone is neutral, we have an opportunity to get to know them sooner, which sometimes results in an "instant best friend" experience. This is especially true when they have an equal sense of non-judgment toward you.

Either way, there is a better, more reliable way to establish a level of comfort with someone when you first encounter them. That is to consciously suspend any judgment about them, no matter what they look like, sound like or are doing when you encounter them. Until you actually meet them and engage with them, you have no idea of who they are or what's going on for them at that moment.

> *When you place a value on a person, you separate yourself from them with a distance in direct proportion to your perception of them as being of greater or lesser value than you.*

To suspend any judgment in the first moments you encounter someone is to allow something deeper…something more meaningful…to come forward that might have a positive impact on both of your lives. You have to be reasonable and use discernment about this, of course, but with increasing awareness of yourself and how you form opinions, you will improve your ability to use discernment and your intuition as you continue to discover how this works.

This was especially true in my time in prison when I was moved from place to place for the first year and half. As a federal prisoner, I could be transferred from one part of the country to another at any given moment without warning, for no apparent reason. It could come at 3:00 a.m., which it did several times, and there would be no indication about where I was going or why. Whatever I couldn't stuff into a small shirt pocket or convince the officers was legal material had to be left behind in the hopes that a cell mate might get my things mailed off to a family member because harried and oftentimes indifferent correctional officers would not always see to it.

Fortunately, I knew about these injunctions before my entrance into the prison system, so I was able to apply a sort of radar in assessing the basic character of the inmates I encountered. That's not an easy thing to do in a prison environment where even a wrong facial expression or misspoken comment can trigger hostile reactions very quickly. It worked for me, however. In several instances, strong friendships formed that enabled me to survive the experience as I became more familiar with unspoken rules about how, and how not, to communicate with other inmates.

One of the most valuable first lessons for me in suspending judgment in prison came from meeting Big Jim, about whom I wrote earlier. Had I formed a judgment about him before we talked, I never would have had a chance to learn lessons and insights from him that ultimately enabled me to not only survive the experience, but to transform it into what it is today. He, and others like him that I encountered along the way, helped me better understand how we can be our own worst enemies and self-saboteurs by how we form judgments about others.

Pre-judgment skews everything, even if you're not obvious about it or conscious of it. People can feel it, no matter how well you think you might be disguising it. The same thing applies in reverse if you're judging someone else as better than you. They feel you diminishing yourself or acting small. Either way, it's disempowering. It causes awkwardness, discomfort, mental or emotional resistance and self-rejection. This is especially true when rejection isn't even an issue, but rather is something only being perceived or projected outward by you without substance or cause.

This doesn't mean opening yourself to everyone without some degree of discernment, but it does mean allowing yourself to be surprised by being willing to suspend pre-disposed opinions or negative anticipation about someone before you know anything about them. I've had stimulating conversations and played chess with highly intelligent men that by their menacing appearance I would have been inclined to cross the street to avoid passing them on a sidewalk in the outside world.

In one instance, I became friends with a particularly intimidating individual who had heard about my work with other inmates on GED preparation. He was confrontative to me with his immense size, scars and tattoos, and an attitude to go with it. Once we began talking without his buddies around to complicate things, we had a great conversation.. Once he was comfortable with me, he told me about his childhood and seeing his father killed over a drug deal, and his mother working as a prostitute. Tears actually welled up in his eyes at one point, and for just a moment I could see the scared little boy hiding inside of him. This was not an uncommon experience for me once the word got around that I was a "standup" guy. What could have been a fateful outcome in my time incarcerated was avoided as I continued to practice suspending judgment about anyone, while at the same time learning to also use a healthy amount of discernment.

The Second Injunction is to Not Compare – which means specifically not comparing yourself to others. Comparison for the sake of self-improvement or inspiration is fine, but the need a lot of people have to value themselves relative to their perceived worth of others is counter-productive and can be easily misleading. It's really just another form of judgment, but bears identifying here because it's often subtle and almost always self-deceptive. More often than not, we tend to project outward toward others what we think they are thinking or perceiving about us. I have seen hostile arguments and even fights break out between men and even a few women over a misperception of something said or done, or even *appearing* to have been said or done.

Once I had to see a personal banker who was busy with an elderly woman at her desk, so I took a seat by the window where there was a courtesy phone for use by waiting customers. The banker got up at one point and took some of the woman's papers to verify something while I decided to use the phone to call a friend. It was a bad connection, so I said "Hello?" a couple of times in a raised voice. Each time I did, the woman at the desk turned and glared at me fiercely…enough that I felt it was unreasonable. When I hung up the phone, she glared at me again and I almost snapped at her but thought better of it and simply asked her if there was something wrong.

"Oh, no," she replied apologetically. "I thought you were talking to me, but I couldn't see you because of the sun glaring behind you. So sorry…"

I was embarrassed to have jumped to a conclusion about her and explained what I was doing, which created a sort of conversation until the banker returned. The banker was a lady friend of mine, and nodded approvingly in my direction. She handed the woman her documents and wished her well, then motioned for me to take the now empty seat.

"Isn't it a shame about Helen," she said, assuming that I knew the woman.

"Oh?" I said. I don't really know her. What happened?"

"Well, her husband of 53 years just had a heart attack yesterday, and passed away. She was here trying to sort things out because he always took care of everything."

That isn't necessarily an example of making comparisons, but it bears mentioning here because of the ease with which we can misperceive things and project on others what we're thinking or feeling. I've thought about that incident many times since then, and tried to imagine the needless added pain it would have caused her had I treated her rudely because I had wrongly assumed that she was glaring at me "fiercely." It's so easy for us to jump to conclusions or to project onto others what we think they are thinking about us, when the chances are they may not be thinking anything about us at all.

Projections like that and jumping to conclusions are often the result of feeling inadequate (inferior), or of feeling superior to others. Either dynamic sets one up for failure because there is always going to be someone better and always someone inferior to you. Either way, you lose the opportunity to gain from the experience you could have had if you had remained neutral. I have experienced the best of both, and what I consider in some cases, the worst of both. Some people who I thought would be immensely helpful to me in my work because of their material wealth and their praise of my work turned out to be what are called "user/takers," and either did nothing or actually used deception to take much-needed resources (money) for their own purposes. Conversely, and much to my surprise and delight, several people who at first appeared to be unlikely to have any financial ability to assist me with my work, became some of my best and least demanding supporters.

> ... the need that most people have to value themselves relative to their perceived worth of others is counter-productive and often obsessive.

The same dynamics as discussed about judgment apply to making comparisons, and it's important to learn to recognize when you do it. The more you can observe the way you interact with others, and them with you, the more you will notice how often you ride a sort of roller coaster of emotions that lead ultimately to either ego-inflation or self-deprecation. This process continues for many people their entire lifetimes, and they never learn why things don't work out for them. The degree to which you can suspend comparing yourself to and judging others is the degree to which you will discover amazing and valuable things about yourself…and them.

Another example of projection and mis-perception (comparison) is when I was in a large detention center in Florida during my pre-trial phase of my detention. It was a large, fortress-like structure of some fourteen stories, each story of which was comprised of four cellblocks facing a central observation post called a "tower." Three times a day, all four cellblocks were called to "chow," at which time the doors of all four opened and everyone filed into the main hallway and were lead off to the dining room where we were directed to sit wherever the officers instructed us.

Several days in a row, I noticed a young man from one of the other cellblocks who wore his hair pinned in many little braids. For some reason, I felt put off by him and avoided contact with him. One day, he and I sat directly across from one another three times in a row. During breakfast, I was surprised to observe him putting his hands over his plate as if to bless his food, and then to quietly say what appeared to be a prayer to himself. When he did it again at lunch, I began to think differently about him. As we stood in line waiting to file back to our cellblocks, we started a conversation. In that short time, and again at dinner that evening, we established that I planned to write a book about my experiences, and that he was an aspiring artist.

> *You never know who will appear in your life as a result of your willingness to see and treat people differently.*

A few days later, he purposefully got in line with me as we were about to leave the dining room, and very deftly handed me a rolled-up piece of paper behind our backs where we wouldn't be observed. I was very nervous not knowing what it was, or if it would get me into trouble, but by that point I had come to trust him just enough to be willing to go along with it, and slid the paper up into my sleeve. When I got back to my bunk, I pulled it out and opened it. It was a magnificent drawing of an eagle with its wings outstretched as if to take to the air, with one of its legs in shackles, but with the other end of the shackle opened. "For the cover of your book," he had written below it. I was stunned. The next day, I looked for him to thank him, but he was gone. I never saw him again.

> *"Don't let your education (mind) interfere with your learning."*
> – Mark Twain

You never know what, or who, will appear in your life as a result of your willingness to see and treat people differently, and to be willing also to show up differently, and more transparently, in their lives.

The Third Injunction is Delete the Need to Understand. This is difficult for people who tend to be more intellectual, but notice the word, *need*. I had a hard time with this one because I happen to be one of those who has to figure everything out. What's important about this injunction is that deleting the need to understand doesn't mean you can't or shouldn't know or understand things, but rather that you stop trying to figure everything out. Drop the *need* to know, which often becomes more important than the learning, and interferes with that happening. The more one is willing to let go of need to know everything, the more his or her intuition comes into play. In writing that, an amusing yet poignant expression attributed to Mark Twain comes to mind, which is "Don't let your education interfere with your learning." For the purpose of this writing, I would change "education" in that expression to "mind," which I believe is what he was referring to.

The entire process of our growth and learning is influenced by how the mind tries to control everything, while the heart (more commonly referred to in recent studies as the "heart-mind") is suppressed. I listened to an interview recently of a medical doctor who has done considerable research on this subject and I was startled at how clearly he presented his findings. According to him, studies have proven that heart cells have a type of neuro-network and is actually capable of processing thought patterns, and *in fact,* better than the brain. It's just that there aren't nearly as many of them as there are in the brain. That's why, the doctor explained, we commonly refer to our hearts when speaking to others in affectionate or emotional ways. 'Hence, the expression, "What does your heart tell you?"'

Carl Jung wrote about the conscious and the unconscious mind – the former being how most of us process our thoughts during our adult years, and the latter being much more vast and untapped knowledge…a sort of "reservoir" of deeper awareness that's available to us if we're willing to cultivate it. This is a different "conscious" and "unconscious" than I've been writing about, which has to do with being mindful and aware, versus being "asleep" or unaware.

In this regard, the conscious mind is what most people perceive as "reality," while the unconscious mind is considered more illusionary. In fact, according to advanced thinkers and researchers of the human mind, it's the other way around. It's like seeing something through a movie or television camera, as one mentor of mine described it. "The conscious mind," he would say, "only sees what the lens of the camera shows, while all around the camera is the reality of what isn't seen visually – everything around and behind the camera lens."

Deleting the need to understand quiets the mind and enables one to step outside of the very limited way one learns to evaluate and judge everything and everyone that the mind perceives as "reality." It allows one to perceive more than just what's in view. There is far more information and other resources available on different levels when one opens deeply enough, including what most people call "coincidence." Most coincidences are not coincidences at all, but are a part of one's creative imagination and openness to other possibilities. The linear mind sees such chance occurrences as "coincidence," while the deeper mind sees them as an alignment of matching possibilities. This is where intuition plays a much more active role, once one learns to trust it and use it more often. Practices such as meditation, yoga and calming the constant mental processing that goes on incessantly in our minds are some ways to access that "reservoir," and develop more of our intuition and "inner knowing."

During early childhood, learning more practical approaches to life is important for survival. It serves us well in learning how to use the mind, but in adulthood it tends to not only get in the way of truth and reality, it actually can distort and block certain truths from being correctly perceived. The mind is powerful, and is trained from birth to judge everything as being potentially harmful or helpful. Unfortunately, in present society, we learn to rely on the mind entirely, and what's directly perceived by it rather than to rely on our feelings – *intuitional* feelings – not emotional ones. Relying solely on the mind and one's linear perceptions sets a person up for inaccuracy, self-inflation or deprecation, and missed opportunities.

I encourage you to experiment on your own. Keep track of your experiences and objectively notice when you are judging, comparing, or trying to figure things out. Be aware of things you do, say and experience, and follow their development. Allow yourself to be surprised. Don't analyze. Just observe, and you may begin to notice patterns. By "keeping track," I don't necessarily mean actually writing things down, although that would be helpful if you can be that organized and diligent. Essentially, just make mental note of such things and you'll improve the technique over time.

You can take it a step further by doing something kind for someone you don't particularly like without them noticing you're doing anything. Pick someone you have to see on a regular basis, and you'll have a chance to observe a gradual and possibly dramatic difference in that person's attitude. We experimented with this in prison, as I wrote in an earlier chapter, and I learned later on that it has to do with a chemical release into the body of a hormone called serotonin. Serotonin makes the recipient of a good deed or kind act feel better – such as a visit from a loved one, or an encouraging letter, or something that causes the person to feel valued and appreciated. Surprisingly, researchers have found that when someone does a good deed for someone else, not only does the serotonin level of the recipient go up, but it also does in the person doing the kind act. Even more surprisingly, they discovered that the serotonin level also goes up in those *observing* the good deed or the kind act. That's especially true, and has been tested in theaters, where audiences viewed romantic and inspirational movies.

Think about good movies you've seen, or how you feel when someone does something heroic or magnanimous toward others. Think about how you feel when someone remembers your name, or goes to the trouble of acknowledging your birthday, or some small thing you like. It's very real stuff, however. As we embrace the fundamentals of suspending judgment of others, comparing ourselves to others and letting go of the need know everything, we will be happier, calmer, and far more aware of how things and people impact us. Even in prison – concrete as well as mental and emotional – we can reach a point of amazement at how simple it is to see how we weave the tangled webs of our lives, once we understand how unknown forces work on us our entire lives.

To the degree that we can do that, we will have richer, deeper and more impactful relationships that are more consistent and long lasting – people who would truly mourn your passing, and who, each time you meet them, make you feel good whenever you're around them. It's not just them, or their good-naturedness that feels good to you. It's your openness to them, and your willingness to trust the process and act accordingly. To the extent that each of us can understand and experiment with just these three things, we can gradually improve the world we live in because we will be making better, more powerful and meaningful changes in the way we do things. Compounded by the rapidly growing number of people in the world who are waking up to the need and benefit of cooperation and collaboration, we can bring about truly civilized communities, nations and humanity overall.

CHAPTER TEN

Compassion

Compassion in its purest form is one of the greatest attributes of the human spirit. It can disarm even the most threatening of people because it is among the most impactful of all human emotions. It is Love at its purest and deepest form. It cuts through the illusions and misguided notions that filter and distort our perceptions of others. One can feel compassion because it's genuine. You can't fake it. You can fake sympathy, but not compassion. Sympathy is often superficial. Compassion runs much deeper. Compassion is love in action…true caring, and willingness to be present for someone else, no matter what they say or do. It compels a similar response in the other person, even if it's just to enable them to receive generous caring. It works on the recipient as well as on those who merely observe compassion in action…just like I wrote about Serotonin.

> *Compassion is love in action… true caring, and willingness to be present for someone else, no matter what they say or do.*

In *The Book of Reconciliation,* published by the Terma Company in Santa Fe, New Mexico, an American writer living in Japan

Compassion

experienced an act of compassion that transformed an entire subway car full of tired Japanese workers. At one stop, a very burly and disheveled man entered the car in which the writer was sitting toward the back. It was obvious the man had been drinking, and he smelled terrible. He rudely pushed his way through the people standing near the door, and treated everyone badly…particularly the women. His rudeness and his odor was so overwhelming it made the writer grow angry, and ready to confront the man even though the man outweighed him by at least a hundred pounds.

Just at the point where the writer was about to step up and confront the man, a small, seemingly frail old man spoke up from across the car sharply enough to get the burly man's attention. Everyone went quiet. The bully looked at the old man at first with surprise, then bewilderment. The old man spoke again, and the big man looked uncertain, then quieted. The old man continued, then stood up and went to the big man and embraced him. In the next few minutes, the raging man was on his knees, sobbing uncontrollably while the old man stroked his hair. The "bully," as it turned out, had just lost his wife and entire family in a car accident, and he had come from a bar where he'd gone from the hospital to drown his sorrow. Everyone in the subway car was transformed from frightened, indignant victims to compassionate onlookers as the old man gently stroked the grieving man's head. That old man had much more than sympathy for the troubled man. He had wisdom enough to know there was something more to the man's problem than simply drinking too much.

Wisdom, which comes from experience, turned fear and anger into compassion, which altered the course of events from something that could have become severely confrontational and even hostile, into something transformative. Had it happened in New York City or Los Angeles, it could have proven fatal to the man, or at least landed him in jail on top of his grief. That act of compassion on the part of the old man may have saved the man's life, and it changed attitudes and perceptions of everyone in the car.

I've never forgotten that story. Even I, as a reader of the story many years after it happened, felt transformed to some degree from the mere reading of the story. That's the power of true compassion.

One never knows another person's burdens and sorrows unless they take the time to listen…really listen… before reacting or judging prematurely. One would hardly expect to find compassion in such a typically uncaring, impersonal environment as a crowded subway in Japan, or New York, or anywhere that large crowds of people are jammed into small spaces. Yet the old man's willingness to see beyond the threats, hostility and imposing figure of a "bully," and feel something deeper and know the pain of a man who was lost and alone, enabled the entire crowd of onlookers to experience something transformative.

> *One never knows another person's burdens and sorrows unless they take the time to listen before reacting or judging prematurely.*

Compassion is not just a passive thing, such as sympathy or remorse. It doesn't require specific action to be taken, but is itself active. It's action just by its impact on others. It compels people to do, think, and speak differently. Mother Theresa was one of the greatest examples of compassion in action. She was a force of nature made real by her constant demonstration of deep caring for the suffering of the sick and dying. Her very nature compelled people to take action to do something about suffering in the world, and her "ministry" grew beyond anything that anyone, including her, could have imagined.

I once watched a Native American medicine man give a ceremonial blessing at the opening of an art gallery – not the sort of circumstances under which one would expect a true medicine man to be doing spiritual work. He was dressed in full Native American ceremonial regalia, and he made sure everyone present was aware of all aspects of the nature of his ceremonial blessing. He made certain each person touched the feathers he was using, and understood the nature of the sage he was about to burn to purify the air around the gallery. It was clear in his eyes and by his respectful nature toward every person that he truly cared about each of them. He exhibited the essence of compassion, which in this case amounted to a deeper and more profound sense of respect than I would expect to see or observe in a commercial setting like that. It was so powerfully done, it could have just as well been a gathering of tribesmen at an ancestral gathering.

I was amazed as I looked around the room and noticed the positive impact he was having even with onlookers who happened by, and watched from a distance. There was such an air of mutual respect and admiration that it lasted for hours. Many people stayed after, and mingled with warmth and caring I had not experienced in any of them before, and I knew many of them. I was deeply moved by the experience, and approached the medicine man afterward. We've met several times since then, and have set an intention to work together in prisons to assist inmates in learning the importance of respecting themselves and others.

What might grow out of that experience will have powerful and long-lasting impact on many people who think their lives don't matter, and therefore they can justify doing anything they choose to do in order to "survive." I've often wondered how many others have been touched by this man's work, and what ripple effect may have been generated by him that may still affect people to this day.

Compassion is a deeper level of respect. It's not conditional on anything, even that it be properly received. It's an honoring of all forces playing on any given situation in one's life. It has no judgments, criticisms, or need for a particular outcome. It's a recognition and acceptance of circumstances that exist at a point in time, and has no expectations of anything. The feeling that comes to a person when he or she knows another person can be actually listening to them is transformative, and can change even the most confronting and hostile of circumstances.

> *Compassion is a deeper level of respect. It's not conditional on anything... even that it be "properly" received by anyone.*

In the film, *Schindler's List*, which was based upon actual events in Nazi Germany during the Holocaust, Schindler's compassion for the Jews in his employ was a good example of what I'm talking about. His compassion was so strong he was able to convince the psychotic commandant he would be a much more powerful man if he "granted life" to the Jews instead of killing them. He put his life on the line with that one act, and ran the risk of alienating a man who could have just as easily taken everything away from him and thrown him in with the rest.

In similar fashion, the movie, *The Green Mile,* demonstrated the power of compassion as the force that enabled the guards to work safely among convicted killers, even in the rare circumstance when it was ignored or abused. Compassion is a realization of the nature of one's humanity…our connection with one another, and to a divine origin. It empowers all parties involved because it brings with it a certain calmness and acceptance of common circumstances that transcend for the moment the more obvious and physical nature of things. If allowed, compassion flows naturally from the core of one's soul. It knows the cause of any disruption or imbalance, and even though it doesn't itself bring specific remedies, it calms emotions and removes impediments to resolving problems.

> *Compassion is a realization of the nature of one's humanity… one's connection with one another, and to a divine origin.*

It instills a sense of trust and honoring such that resolving tensions and hostility becomes more attainable. I remember vividly many instances where someone acted toward me with compassion when I was facing situations where I thought there was no resolution. I recall how impactful it was when I realized that my life meant something to someone else. In a much simpler and often overlooked way, I often notice motorists in my very heavily-trafficked community waiting to merge into the lineup, and when I paused to let them in, the look of relief on their faces. That's compassion of a lesser degree, and yet the momentary positive impact on their faces was no less rewarding and satisfying. Hopefully, I think each time I do that it encourages a pattern of people passing the act of kindness along to others.

Compassion doesn't judge, compare, quantify, or qualify anything. It doesn't care about what happened, who did what to whom, or what any of the circumstances surrounding a given situation or event might be. It simply recognizes that someone or something is out of balance and needs kindness and caring without criticism, blame, outrage or reaction.

The ability to put oneself into others' shoes is a form of compassion, and provides one with a far more intelligent and effective means of dealing with a given problem. To the extent that one is able to get outside of himself or herself in dealing with others, one can first feel, then see a more creative and effective approach. That way, the other party will be more open to listening because they feel more cared about and respected. One can feel compassion for someone who commits a crime or an offense against another, even while administering punishment for those offenses just as portrayed in the movie *The Green Mile*. Acting compassionately toward someone who has done something wrong or committed a crime doesn't condone their actions or sympathize with them. It merely shows respect for their existence on the planet.

Recent television documentaries and news articles related to gang members and even notorious gang leaders who have changed their thinking and behavior are tremendous examples of how that can work. Despite considerable bloodshed and violence that has characterized many of these people's lives, it is a powerful source for significant and broad-based societal change when those who have lived by the codes of gang behavior take a huge, personal risk in disavowing those codes, and courageously offering guidance away from it. This comes at great peril to them, and with tremendous skepticism and resistance on the part of authorities. But such is the nature of the human experience at this time in history – all the more reason for compassion to be cultivated and promoted in every way possible. It needs to come first on an individual basis, then outwardly toward others until enough people are acting compassionately such that it becomes the norm, rather than anger, indignation, or retribution that never results in anything positive in the long run.

Never think your own acts of compassion won't amount to anything, or that they don't have value. Everything matters, and it can be the single most significant factor in changing someone's life for the better just as it happened with the drunken man on the Tokyo subway, or with that group of people in the gallery. The more you can incorporate some act of compassion into your daily living, the more you will ultimately see a change in attitudes of others around you in ways you may not know if you were a part of it. You *are* a part of it, and even the tiniest contribution to others is ultimately noted on some grander scale, even as every note played on every instrument in a symphony orchestra is part of the music heard by even the undiscerning ear.

The Conductor knows if it's played right, and to an increasing degree as you continue to "practice" doing it, you will also know… which is all that really matters.

As a personal note from me to each reader, I want to emphasize how important it is right now that we all take personal responsibility for how we choose to interact with each other…with compassion and openness to different points of view. That does not mean condoning or agreeing with perversity, radicalism or demeaning attitudes and behavior. It means being willing to consider others' points of view, and how they show up in the world. By acting as the old man did in the Tokyo subway, you give them a chance to feel as if they matter, and that you aren't in opposition to them even if you feel differently than they do.

That's the nature of compassion. It's not weak or vacillating, but rather it's strong and unwavering in caring about what really matters. We matter...all of us...and that's what that old man demonstrated with the drunken man that broke through his agony and blindness from the tragedy he was dealing with. Compassion doesn't care about extremism, or right vs left. It only shines a light on whatever the circumstances are so that all involved can see things more clearly...if they're willing to. That's the key...we must be willing to see the bigger picture...from others' points of view. In their shoes, so to speak.

Compassion is no weak or fickle thing. It's Divine Love... whatever form you believe "Divinity" to be. It honors life and human existence as sacrosanct, and as such, it is one of the most powerful forces in the Universe. Call it whatever you like, it's the fierce Love that Mother Theresa, Gandhi, Martin Luther King and Nelson Mandela exhibited, and it's what is needed in the world now. And a lot of it. We can't wait for another person like that to appear. *We* need to appear...each in our own way. It has to be steadfast and unconditional. It's about strength of a different kind that doesn't need chest-beating or saber-rattling or guided missiles and flags waving. It's strength of caring about each other...real caring, no matter what. With that, we can restore decency and respect to our world.

"True detachment isn't a separation from life but the absolute freedom within your mind to explore living."

– Ron W. Rathbun

CHAPTER ELEVEN
Detachment

Each of the preceding chapters has one common theme, which is personal freedom – freedom from old beliefs and conditioned thinking that while some or even all of it may have served a useful purpose at one point in our lives, constrain us as we grow older, and limit our ability to think and act in a more liberating way to become better and more self-empowered. Another principle, or value, that I have mentioned in earlier chapters but want to bring more clearly to your attention in this chapter is detachment.

Detachment does not mean indifference or not caring about something or someone important to you, but rather to be willing to allow things to take place and unfold in a more natural way. There is a type of paradox that I have learned over the years regarding detachment, which is that while it is important to have a desire and a vision of your goals and to do everything reasonable that is possible for you to achieve those goals and vision, it is also important for you to be willing to be in a state of mind that allows for a given outcome rather than to make it, or force it, to happen. This can be pretty tricky business in a world of materialism where acquiring things and having a big bank balance are driving forces in most people's lives. I'm not saying that it's bad or wrong to want things and to achieve material goals. What I'm saying is that it's more important to release the need for a certain outcome, and allow for something more natural to occur that might be even better than you had hoped for.

Detachment is an easy thing to talk about and to believe you are "detached" from an outcome. However, talking and thinking about detachment, and actually *being* detached, are entirely different things.

> *Detachment does not mean indifference or not caring, but rather to be willing to allow things to unfold in a more natural way.*

We grow up wanting things, and we are constantly influenced by friends, family, teachers, television, billboards, magazines and movies to acquire things – materially, psychologically and emotionally – and the pressure to "keep up with the Jones'" makes giving any of it up nearly impossible. I'm not suggesting that you give anything up, but rather give up the *need* to have it a certain way.

If you can get yourself into a mindset that it doesn't really matter if you don't accumulate material things and money, yet at the same time work mindfully toward achieving the goals that really matter is a delicate dance to perform. But it enables you to achieve more than what you first set out to accomplish without the emotional or psychological stress of having to accumulate things, which often leads to obsessive or dysfunctional behavior. But detachment can be a difficult state of mind to achieve.

The reason for the difficulty is that people are commonly too attached to their beliefs about things and people in their lives to want to change themselves very much. For many people, changing even a little bit is scary because in order to change, there is a strong tendency to feel like they're admitting they have been wrong. Worse, it might mean losing relationships with some people because changing often means "waking up," which causes one to re-think their relationships and why they're in them in the first place. By that, I mean all relationships…friends, spouses, familial, etc. That kind of change often requires changing the unspoken rules that keep people stuck in old behavior patterns with each other. To change those rules often means that some relationships will have to go because they won't serve any useful purpose any longer. You wanting change in your life doesn't mean that others will also.

There is a story that circulates among schools of thought and human growth seminars and workshops that may or may not be true, but serves as a good example. A man walking down an ocean pier where various fishermen and women are selling their catches for the day, spots a man who has live crabs in a fairly shallow basket. He inquires why the man uses such a shallow basket and why the crabs don't all escape. "They are too busy holding each other back to escape," says the fisherman, with a smile. And so it is with us humans, seminar facilitators point out dramatically. Psychologically and emotionally, we don't really want to change, and we aren't real comfortable with our friends and family members changing, either.

The biggest obstacle to getting people to accept the importance of detachment is their attachment to being right, or "realistic," as they will most often say in defending their beliefs. They're not about to change those beliefs. They've got entire lifetimes of experience to prove they are right, even if it means ongoing discomfort, misery, and continuous failed relationships. Familiarity, as many human growth teachers and counselors often point out, is more compelling than transformation, even if it's uncomfortable on a continual basis. It's like a pair of shoes that don't fit quite right, yet we continue to wear them because we're used to them. We are creatures of habit – often to an extreme – and attachment is a habit pattern that is almost impossible for many people to break, even when one really, *really* wants to. Often, it takes a calamity or a cathartic experience to get someone's attention enough to even recognize that they have a dysfunctional habit, let alone to be willing to change it.

How many times do you hear "love hurts" from people who continuously create dysfunctional relationships that always end up hurting them? Or that someone who constantly finds themselves having accidents is "accident prone"? That's because they are attached to their beliefs about how life works, or, in their case, doesn't work. Love "hurts" those who believe it does because they hold onto that belief as an expected outcome, even as they profess to want all the joy and happiness love is "supposed" to bring. So, they do things and say things throughout the relationship in anticipation of being hurt, and – lo and behold – that's exactly what happens. They sabotage the relationship, blame the other person, and add one more "proof" to their long list of experiences that reinforces the notion that love, in fact, *always* hurts.

Does that mean a person can't create a loving relationship that never hurts? Not necessarily. We all have our faults and shortcomings, and emotions get bruised pretty easily. I know I haven't had an entirely pain-free relationship history. I'm human, and I have emotions and past memories that have often caused me to make poor choices in relationships that I wasn't even aware that I had. I also have personal preferences about some things that I hold onto in spite of discomfort until they reach the point where I finally am forced to remember it's always my choice to change the way I feel about anything.

No matter how "detached" I think I am at any point, there are times when things just don't work out the way I want them to, and I feel the loss and the lack of the sweetness and fulfillment I want. But then I remember the breakthroughs that always come whenever I let go of how I want things to turn out, and to the degree I truly let go and trust the process that I wrote about previously, circumstances begin to shift noticeably for the better.

> *It's never about the other person or the circumstances involved; it's always the attitude one has about the experience.*

I've been through enough relationships of all kinds by now to know I create every experience I have, and I alone am in charge of how each one comes out. The less I try to force the outcome the way I want it to be, the better it comes out – very often to my surprise and delight. I made the decisions that led to the creation of the experience, and I am the one person in charge of the mechanism that determines the outcome, which is my attitude. It's never about the other person or about the circumstances involved in any given event. If I'm involved in it, it's always ultimately about me and the attitude I have about what comes of the experience. Of course, the other person and the other aspects of any experience are significant, and contribute to it, but I am the one who is responsible for how I created and handled my part of the experience.

Detachment

There is a mystery about detachment that determines the successful, or unsuccessful, outcome of any experience. That is how well you can balance detachment from the outcome with taking responsibility for how and why you created and handled that experience. That applies equally to a one-time, passing experience such as a car accident, a lost wallet or a one-night stand, as it does to a long-term relationship such as a marriage, committed relationship, or business partnership. The degree to which you fully embrace and accept your choices and responsibility for your actions in any circumstance, *balanced with* your willingness to let go of the need to control any of it or to hold onto an expected outcome, will be the degree to which you will experience liberation from a negative outcome.

Does that mean you can't control your experiences? No, it doesn't. It just means that you let go of the *need* to control it. In Chapter Nine, the mystery of Understanding was explained as something that comes more easily the more willing one is to let go of the need to understand. That need we have to figure everything out, or the need to control a given situation, relationship, or outcome is the stumbling block. It's the *need* that gets in our way, and prevents us from seeing something or feeling something intuitively that is within our grasp all the time. Where it gets problematic is in our emotions.

Most of us are emotionally driven. We may intellectualize our way through life, and we may have college degrees that say we are mentally accomplished and pragmatic decision-makers, but at our core many of us make decisions based upon observations and experiences that are emotionally based. Time and again, I hear of situations where, in spite of the best "well-laid" plans, a relationship fell apart or a promising business venture failed. Why? Largely because unresolved emotions and personal ego attachment were at the core of key decisions and behaviors, which resulted in somebody sabotaging the experience.

Most people, to varying degrees, are scared to death that something's going to go wrong, so they build their lives and their attitudes based upon self-protection and, to a large extent, self-indulgence. Many even take that to another level, which is self-delusion, and if left undetected or uncorrected long enough, ultimately to self-destruction. No small number of famous celebrities and once-wealthy socialites died empty and alone – many at their own hands, or from addictions – which is a sad testament to this truth. I have encountered several people in retirement homes and convalescent centers who had amassed fortunes, built cities and climbed to the heights of success only to end up sitting alone in wheelchairs, gazing forlornly out at the world where they once had thrived.

> *The mystery about success is in going after what you want, and letting go of how you think they have to come out.*

How, then, does one deal with the apparent paradox of, on the one hand, wanting something and, on the other, letting go of it? Isn't wanting something the driving force behind achieving certain goals that lead to having it? Yes, of course. It's essential that you have desires, or nothing of any consequence would ever take place in your life. In fact, it's important that you identify what you really want, and passionately go after it with everything you've got.

The mystery about achieving success, however, is in being willing to let go of things coming out exactly the way you think they have to come out. I realize that I wrote that previously, but this is so important it bears repeating: This doesn't mean they won't or can't. In fact, the more you hold the vision of what you want in your imagination, and be willing at the same time to let go of the need to have it that way, the more it may fit perfectly with the way you pictured it – perhaps even better than you pictured it. It takes practice, and trust unlike anything you most likely have ever experienced, but it works every time. It may not always appear like it does, but given time and a broader perspective, it will. It just may not come "packaged" the way we want. We do ourselves a great disservice when we think we are powerless to do anything to overcome difficulties in our lives, or we think we have to force a given outcome.

In Richard Bach's best-selling book, *Illusions: Adventures of a Reluctant Messiah,* there is a "parable," as he terms it, in which he uses the metaphor of creatures in a "great, crystal river," at the bottom of which they all cling desperately to the rocks along the bottom. One of them tires of the clinging and tells the others he wants to let go. He wants the freedom to lift himself up above all the clinging and see where the river wants to take him. The others around him exclaim "No!" and try to convince him that to let go will result in his being bashed against the rocks downstream, and will lead to certain death.

He finally decides that even death would be better than spending his life clinging, so he lets go. Sure enough, he *is* bashed against the rocks – again and again. But he refuses to cling again, and in the process he learns to ride the current and lifts himself free. All the creatures downstream look up and see him "flying" above them, and declare he is the "new messiah" come to set them free. But still none are willing to let go.

The same theme is carried out in his classic book preceding that one, *Jonathan Livingstone Seagull*, a simple yet profound and beautiful tale of a seagull who refuses to grovel over bits of garbage and fish heads, and chooses instead to use his wings to discover the art of perfect flight.

Simplistic as those stories may be, they are profound in their application to human existence. It's no different, except that we just act out our stories in a more elaborate and self-deceptive manner. We don't even realize how we cling to our "rocks," or "grovel for our food." We may live in nice houses and dine in fine restaurants, but if we aren't happy and at peace with ourselves, we're really just clinging and groveling in our own human way. It's quite simple, but it's not necessarily easy. It's difficult to see it, let alone change it, because it requires changing habits and doing things against one's nature, or, rather, against one's conditioned beliefs and deeply ingrained habits.

The other side of the detachment equation is taking responsibility not just for one's actions, but for one's thinking and feelings. If you want to change your life, as the philosopher Fra Giovanni put it back in the 16th century, you must change your *thinking*. That advice is even more true today. Our minds are the finest computers ever created, however they are only as good as the information we program into them and how we use them. We learn from birth that we aren't "good enough," or that "there isn't enough," or that we have to be tenacious and competitive. Competition and tenacity are fine under certain circumstances, but not when they control your life or bring harm to others who might be weaker. Tenacity is often used to compliment someone's stick-to-itiveness, however to me it's not

Detachment

necessarily a virtue. In fact, it's more often than not just another level of stubbornness that doesn't always lead to one's fulfillment. Take it from someone who made it a near art form. It's one of the more common traits friends of mine use to describe me, and I cringe whenever I hear it. I've learned the hard way that it isn't always going to get you what you want if you don't take other things into consideration along the way. You may think it's leading there, but you will likely only wind up at the top of a mountain peak you hadn't planned on, and then you have to go back down and start all over again on the one you intended to climb.

> *Life's lessons don't get easier as you grow; they get harder...but if you're paying attention, you get through them quicker.*

A better metaphor might be that I always prided myself in being able to "move mountains," only to find out later in life that mountains are where they are for a reason. They don't need to be moved.

Another important thing to learn about detachment, as with the other core values I've written about, is that just because you are learning to use them to make improvements in your life doesn't mean that the challenges necessarily get any easier. On the contrary, they often get *harder*. But the good news, a very wise woman told me once when I was lamenting about life's hard lessons, is that "we get through them quicker." I had to smile when she said it as she sipped on her glass of wine, and I still smile now when I think of the irony of the statement and what challenges came up for both of us in the next several weeks. As we continue to strengthen our understanding of these various mysteries I'm writing about, and practice such techniques as detachment and letting go, we do in fact find the ride getting smoother if not quicker. If you're a believer in reincarnation, it makes for a much more promising ride the next time around or, if not, at least a better conclusion to this one.

All the more reason to learn and embrace detachment just as much as you embrace and uphold your desires. They are both equal in importance in manifesting anything. In the process, you will find yourself more in control of your life and happier than you can imagine because you're not wasting time and energy trying to figure everything out or controlling everything.

Does one ever get through with the lessons? I don't know. I think not, but I know without a doubt that everything has a purpose, and mysteries exist for our exploration and discovery of what works and what doesn't. My life's deepest desires and joys have come from trusting the process. I've learned that desire and detachment go hand in hand. I know this to be true because I've discovered more about who I am and what I really want than I could ever learn in textbooks or manuals. Therein lies the truth about what most of us want. It's not "out there," but inside of us for our own discovery and guidance. A bigger part of it is like that creature at the bottom of the great crystal river letting go. When I've let go of the need to have things come out the way I think they should, the ride becomes transformative and far more enjoyable.

"The human spirit is stronger than anything that can happen to it."
– CC Scott

CHAPTER TWELVE
The Human Spirit

Several decades ago, a man by the name of Alvin Toffler wrote a book about the acceleration of technology, and wrote that even the *rate* of acceleration was accelerating to the extent that those of us who were alive back then would not recognize or be able to keep up with the changes that would be happening now. The title of his book was *Future Shock,* and from everything I'm seeing and have experienced just in the past few years, I have to say that he was right. Shock is just what we are experiencing – so much so that shock has become "the new normal," which has become one of the most common expressions in the media and in many private conversations today.

Among the things that stood out the most for me in his futuristic book, one in particular impacted me the most: "Future historians," he wrote rather matter-of-factly, "will look back on this very time as the dividing line between civilized and uncivilized humankind." In so writing, I don't believe he was referring to high-technology, medical advances and scientific breakthroughs. I believe he was referring to what many people and modern teachings refer to as "consciousness," or the increasingly more popular term, "mindfulness."

Call it what you want, I believe Mr. Toffler was referring to an awakened state of awareness that differentiates a "civilized" society from an "uncivilized" one. To me, it has do with how many people have reached a state of becoming aware of the impact they have on each other and the world as a whole, and are doing something proactively about it. That would be as opposed to those who are unaware of such things, and have no interest in or motivation to do anything differently. Whatever Toffler may have meant, "uncivilized" appears to be the present state of our world with extreme polarization and politicization of cultures, pandemics and climate change all combined to give humanity the greatest challenges in its entire history. How much and how many of us are awake enough and willing to take the right steps to do something meaningful, I believe, will determine the positive outcome for humanity…or not, as the case may be.

Never in my lifetime – and many evolved thinkers are saying perhaps in all of human history – has the human species faced the global challenges we face today in nearly every major category affecting our development as a society. I am not an alarmist, neither a doomsayer, and have never been a cynic or a pessimist. Rather, I am an optimist to the core, and have always found something about which to be optimistic no matter how hopeless things might appear to be.

Right now, in the most non-political, unbiased and most practical way I can put this, humanity is facing the most challenging period of its entire existence. Even the most advanced of ancient civilizations did not have the power to disturb the natural forces of Earth, let alone to alter them to the point of threatening our existence as we are doing presently. Truly, even as the die-hard optimist I am, I'm saying if we don't substantially change the way we are living on this planet – and soon – all the signs indicate there is a distinct possibility humanity might not make it through the next few decades.

That said, I'm also saying that as great as the challenges may be, so are the opportunities for us to transform ourselves and create a whole new world that isn't just a line from a popular movie. Truly, as complex and difficult as things may appear to be for us, enough people taking a positive and meaningful direction can yet create a world where people can live and work freely, and with respect for one another and for the planet...the kind of world I alluded to in Chapter One. It's completely up to us –

> *As great as the challenges may be, so are the opportunities for us to transform ourselves and create a whole new world.*

individually and collectively – to make better choices and take meaningful action to change the way things are going right now. It may seem like pure idealism and possibly unrealistic, but many of the greatest transformations in history started off that way. It takes great determination and desire for improvement to bring about the kind of changes that are needed, however there is one critical element we all have access to that can alter the course of even the most "unchangeable," oppressive forces that stand in our way. It's what I refer to as *Human Spirit*.

When the cause is right, and the need is great enough, human beings can access powers beyond their imaginations. We've all heard stories of superhuman feats of strength performed under duress or extreme need. I read of a man attempting to repair something under

The Human Spirit

his car, and the jack collapsed on him. I don't recall who it was, but someone nearby was able to lift up the car enough for others to pull the man out from under the car…and it wasn't a big or muscular man. He didn't even know how he was able to do it. A woman managed to lift a grand piano that had collapsed on her small child, who was then able to crawl out unharmed.

There are many stories of extraordinary feats performed in an emergency. In the Far East, mystics and yogi's can slow their heartbeats and their breath, and remain motionless for days…even weeks…of time considered impossible by the Western world.

Who hasn't seen or heard of men and women who can break concrete blocks with their bare hands? Or walk on beds of red-hot coals? Those aren't feats of visual trickery. They're very real, and we're all able to achieve such a level of consciousness if we really want or need to. Those examples may all be physical, but there is something not so physical that they accessed, and that, I believe, was human spirit. Many people don't believe in it, or even know that it exists, because they rarely see it or feel it unless there is a catastrophe or a sudden dire need. Then, just for the moment, it comes alive long enough to achieve the needed outcome.

On a medical basis, there are many stories of people who outlive the grimmest diagnoses – beyond what medical science says is possible. I read once about a single mother in her forties who was diagnosed with terminal cancer and given only a few months to live. She had a teenage son who was only in the tenth grade of high school, and she said she could not leave him alone until he graduated. The cancer went into remission, but within a few weeks after his graduation it returned with a vengeance and she passed away a short time afterward. Another recent and more astonishing demonstration of our ability to change any outcome was a man who was diagnosed with terminal cancer so advanced that doctors were allowed to use an experimental drug on him. They told him it was experimental, but one doctor told him it had proven to be successful on several patients who were worse off than he was. He believed what the doctor told him, and his cancer went into remission. Before he was released from the hospital, it was determined the drug wasn't the correct one. He found out, and the cancer came back. The doctors were deeply puzzled. Based upon those two events, however, they decided to treat him with essentially a placebo but told him it was the correct drug and, lo' and behold, his cancer went into remission…again. Then, assuming that he would be okay by that point, they told him that it had only been a placebo. To their astonishment and deep regret, the cancer returned with such intensity that the man succumbed within a short time after that.

That's human spirit in action. It's directly connected to our beliefs and desires. It's not some hokey-pokey, mystical magic. It's "The Force"…for real. That's not to take anything away from the Holy Spirit of Christian teachings, which is also very real as long as one believes in it strongly enough, and that's the key. How fervently one believes in something, *and has sufficient desire for a given result,* determines the outcome. It's all a matter of what you believe, and how much you believe it…enhanced and empowered by the principles I've written about in the previous chapters. What's most important at this point is that you know that whatever you believe in – negative or positive – is what will shape your life and your destiny. Unfortunately for those who don't make a commitment to their own awakening and personal growth, and just "go along" with the status quo, life will remain rather drab and pointless no matter how much material or physical gain they might make in their lives.

It won't really matter in coming times how much is in one's bank account or where they live, but rather how much they care about what really matters. That would be discovering and connecting with their own human spirit, and with others who care and are committed to improving life for humanity and the planet. To put it into better perspective, it's like having a beautiful home you have spent much of your life to build, but the home was made with the lowest quality materials that ultimately prove over time to be weak and impossible to replace or repair. What compounds the problem is that so many other people's "homes" were built in the same way, and no amount of money in all the banks will be enough to fix the problem. If you want a graphic, real-life example of what I'm referring to, and not just a metaphor, consider the recent collapse of the luxury condominium tower in Miami. To me, that's what happens to the human body when neglected long enough. They may not always collapse so dramatically, but they do ultimately break down over time.

> *What's most important is that you know that whatever you believe in – negative or positive – is what will shape your life and your destiny.*

Regarding climate change issues, on a much grander scale, it doesn't have to be that way. The worst of it can still be avoided, according to current revised estimates by climate scientists, but we're running out of time. It's going to be that way for a while because we've been collectively unaware and inattentive for too long to what it means to be real and genuine in our personal lives and, outwardly, toward the planet and each other. I'm telling you without hesitation or doubt that we can still turn things around, no matter how difficult things may seem at present. Enough people making the right decisions to improve their thinking and actions, and caring enough to recognize and accept what needs to be done, can turn things around. Miracles happen every day, but we don't always see them. When enough people wake up and start cooperating and collaborating in more positive ways, really big miracles can and will happen.

    I'm reaching the point where I don't use terms such as "consciousness" or "mindfulness" much anymore, although there's nothing wrong with either term. I simply do my best to be more self-aware, and willing to trust in that to get through each day even when external circumstances such as pandemics, political upheaval, climate change and conflict in the world drag me down. I remain aware that I get to choose my attitude each day I get up and, as difficult as it might be to fully embrace at times, it has proven to work for me so many times I cannot deny that I have more control over my life than I once thought.

    There are so many books, articles, seminars, and teachings that have been emerging over the past several decades, one only has to want to know how to make improvements in their lives to begin the process. This book is one such avenue, but it's only an "entry-level" effort, as I joke with my friends. There is so much more available to you if you look. But it might be helpful to you if you know that simply having a sense of true caring and compassion will guide you, and it will grow in strength as you continue to allow it to be your underlying motivation in all thoughts and actions. Caring and compassion will connect you with others who are the same way, and to resources and chance encounters that will surprise and amaze you.

This is what I refer to as the human spirit, upon which I have come to rely in most of my interactions with others. I am not a theologian, a Jungian analyst, or a credentialed anything, but I have been on this Earthly journey for seven decades now, and I have seen and experienced enough by this point to know and believe that I have a soul that embodies that human spirit, and it can be relied upon to get me through anything…if I pay attention, and if I care enough to do the right things with my life. If I don't, it will give me the opposite.

A woman who was one of my first exposures to this realization used to run three-day seminars called "Breakthrough Drama." She was an actress, which might explain the title, but she was exceptionally inspiring once she hit her stride midway into each seminar. She would be talking about "God," the "Soul," "Spirit," and "Consciousness," and she said it's all the same thing. "It's like electricity," she would exclaim. "It doesn't *care*. It'll fry your eggs, or it'll fry your ass. It's up to you how you use it, so pay attention."

It seems like a pretty simple concept, yet try as you will to figure it out, it escapes your grasp. You feel good when you hear about how lives transform from just "letting go and letting God," as people often say, or from "trusting the process," but when you find yourself in an argument with your spouse over trivial matters, or you constantly get cut off in traffic by rude drivers, or another mass shooting erupts somewhere and costs of living keep spiraling out of sight, it's pretty hard to stay in touch with that inner knowing and calm yourself down. Part of the problem is we try too hard to figure it all out, or we're in a state of constant reaction, therefore it escapes our notice when it's been right inside of us all along. We were, in fact, born with it. It's as natural to us in our beginning years as breathing.

It's not some kind of mystical teaching. I was raised a Catholic, studied the Bible with very strict Seventh-Day Adventists, and attended many Lutheran, Presbyterian, Baptist, and Methodist churches in earlier adult years. I had the opportunity to spend a lot of time with devout Mormons, and have come to understand a great deal of Eastern thought and spirituality along the way. Much to my amazement, there is more commonality among all of them than most people realize, and it requires an underlying state of individual awareness to understand why that might be so.

What I've learned about an awakened state of consciousness is nothing that necessarily goes against any Eastern or Western religious or spiritual teachings. An awakened state of consciousness allows us to access human spirit, which involves essentially nothing more than quieting one's mind and allowing for a meditative or, for the religiously inclined, a prayerful state of being. You don't have to sit cross-legged on pillows, burn incense, or surround yourself with crystals or religious statues to achieve a more conscious state of mind. You can do that by listening more carefully within yourself, being more attentive to what's going on there, and cultivating your intuition. Consciousness is, essentially, being "awake" – not to be confused with the current, much-maligned and misused political term, "woke."

By "awake," I don't mean the opposite of sleeping, but rather taking your state of mind at any given moment to a deeper level of awareness. It's paying closer attention than you may have before, and hearing, seeing, and *feeling* at an entirely different level. It's been the basis of this book – the concept that you suspend long-standing beliefs about yourself and your perceptions about the nature of life long enough to see and feel things differently. It means learning to trust your intuition.

Neville Goddard, a true "mystic" and devout Christian, lectured extensively on the subject of consciousness during the 1950's, and had this to say about it: "Consciousness is the only reality, and where you are conscious of *being,* psychologically, determines the circumstances of your life." The Ancients knew this great truth, but many of our modern teachers and theologians seem yet to have discovered or accepted it. Scientists may call it energy, while scripture refers to it as "the Holy Spirit." I won't even try to explain or define or analyze any of that, but rather am only offering a layman's interpretation for now in order to get the basic point across.

Your level of consciousness, or "spirit" or "energy," is where you're at in your mind at any given moment. What's going on in your life is a direct result of your thinking and emotional state, and what you believe. If you believe life is hard, it will be hard. I wrote in an earlier chapter about Ron Heagy ("Roll on, Ron"), who has been confined to a wheelchair for most of his adult life, yet to hear or watch him speak you wouldn't think he was confined at all. If you only saw him from the neck up, you would think he was a totally normal, functioning human being. What's generally going on in Ron's mind is happiness to be alive and functional, despite having none of the abilities most of us have to be comfortable and able to move about freely.

Consciousness has to do not only with your state of mind, but what you consent to...by choice or by habit. You consent to a state of mind either by habit (default), or by conscious choice. You may have to work at it to keep yourself alert and aware, but at least you are more likely to make better choices and decisions as you get more used to it. In the process of doing so, you will become more of an observer of your life rather than merely a passenger in the backseat, so to speak. To be an "observer" doesn't mean not to participate, however. Quite the contrary. To fully engage life on a more conscious level, one must go through each experience physically, mentally and emotionally, but at the same time to pay attention from the "observer" state in order to learn the lessons each experience brings. Without that observer state, one simply repeats the same or similar patterns and activities in much the same fashion, over and over again, year after year, and then often wonders why his or her circumstances never change.

> *Consciousness has to do not only with your state of of mind, but what you consent to... by choice or by habit.*

If you want your life to change, you must determine what you want, what you personally find acceptable, and have consented to as true for you before you can change it. In more common terms, to take stock of who you are and what is really true about you so you'll have a better idea of where to begin. To get a clear sense of what that means, consider how you react to a given situation. By uncritically observing your automatic reaction to an event, person or thing, you have an opportunity to find out just how you really feel on a deeper, more aware state than you might have been able to before. In other words, to be open, objective and truthful with yourself.

As you elect to make changes in your life, you'll find it's not always smooth sailing. As a matter of fact, it might be painful as you come to terms with things that don't quite line up with things and people you've been familiar with for most of your life. Once you start noticing how you react to what goes on around you, you will begin a process that will ultimately reveal who you really are and want to be. As you do that, the circumstances around you will change without you necessarily doing anything visibly. Your relationships will change by necessity because you're changing as you pay closer attention to what's going on inside of you.

Remember in Chapter Seven when I referred to the masks most of us wear? Those are merely a way of hiding our real feelings and our real selves from others. The trouble is, we become so automatic about using those masks we lose track of who we are, and we *become* those masks, as I wrote. That shriveled-up, angry old man who once rode the West as the Lone Ranger on his white stallion was a testament to me of how much we get so caught up in our masks that we rarely figure out why we are so desperate, depressed or angry, lost or alone in the midst of abundance, beauty and opportunity. Those are all a matter of choice of attitude, and your resulting level of consciousness about yourself and how you live and have your being in this world.

Beyond The Chaos — *The Human Spirit*

You can be a preacher, a rabbi, priest, Imam, or medicine man or woman, and also be conscious (awake). In fact, the awakened ones are the best, from what I've experienced. They're alive, alert, and full of inspiration, and they're more open to other philosophies and ideologies. They know who they are, and they're comfortable with themselves. They're also more passionate about life and all events. Anything less to them is unconsciousness, drab and mediocre. None of that is necessarily "bad"… it's just less than what we are capable of becoming while we're on this planet.

> *Once you change the circumstances of your life, your life will steadily improve because you're paying more attention to your choices.*

If you don't like the circumstances of your life, look objectively into the cause or causes, and be willing to be more real with yourself and accept that in one way or another you created those circumstances no matter what they may look or feel like to you. Once you do that, then your consciousness about whatever it was will change because you're more aware of who's responsible. Your life will gradually and steadily improve because you're paying more attention to it. You will have to be strong and determined enough to stick with it, which might mean having to change your circumstances at home. You might have to stop going to that bar down the street on a regular basis, and do something to change your routines at work and with some of your personal relationships and your languaging. That's not easy, and it's statistically the main reasons why people don't really change. In spite of the popularity of the books and movies I've mentioned earlier, people don't always "get it," or have the courage and passion to actually make the changes required.

I'm sure the people who ran the Landmark Forums that proliferated around the country over the last few decades, or who manage Tony Robbins' operations, would have some interesting statistics to report if they kept track of the graduates of their courses. People walk on fire at some of Tony's trainings, which requires a hugely altered state of consciousness. I know. I've done it twice, but not at Tony's, and with no expensive weeklong training. My point has to do with the long-term success of human growth trainings and workshops, and how well people do with what they've learned once they get back home. More often than not, it tends to fade over time. They get back to the same old neighborhood and the same old friends and family members all wanting to know what was so damn important to spend that much money on, or to take that much time to learn. They expect to see something instant, profound or visible, and before very long many seekers are back to their old routines and embarrassed because they don't have anything to show…yet…for their delving into the mysteries of life.

But that's not necessarily true for all of them. Some people go back for more. I did. Quite a bit more. My forums were more business oriented, but they were run by people who were highly aware. I was fortunate to also have attended several that were deeply spiritual and transformative, including the granddaddy of them all, as it turned out – the U.S. Bureau of Prisons. As I wrote earlier, it takes time to turn decades of living into something of greater substance than merely collecting things and being obsessed with bigger, better, faster, sexier, or more opulent.

Watch your reactions to life, people, and events. Any conscious change you can make in the way you look at or react to outer things and events by self-observation and detachment will gradually change your world in some intangible way until, with enough practice, it will become tangible and to some extent even measurable. It's essential that you be willing to be passive in observing "bad" or unacceptable things around you. Not that you shouldn't have negative feelings about something distasteful or repugnant, but in your mind, remain passive, and – I love this term – imperturbable.

> *That which you react to defines and limits you. Change how you react to things, and your life will change accordingly.*

As soon as you can accomplish that state of mind, the negative things in your life will dissipate and diminish. You simply won't be in a reactionary state of mind about anything. You will be objective and measured in your response to them, which is a very different energy than reactionary, which is the most common default attitude for many, if not most of us. It's a more calm state of mind that enables you to make decisions and act in a more reasonable way. That which you react to defines and limits you. Change how you react to things in your life, and your life will change accordingly.

Only by observing your own state of consciousness through your reactions and *responses* in your dealings with others and with the events of your life can you discover the cause of whatever is happening at any point in time. By observing your reactions, you can find your true Self. You are, and you become, all you consent to be by allowing yourself to reflect upon each thing or event, and by how you either react or respond. Think kind and compassionate thoughts, even in the darkest, most difficult moments, and just as every heroic deed or role you read or heard about when you were a kid, your own inner hero will show up in some form just like mine did so outrageously that I could not have predicted it in my wildest imagination.

Finally, never envy someone else's good fortune. You don't know about their secret struggles, or what misfortunes they have been through or that might befall them yet. Just work on yourself, and find your true Self...your Soul, if you will. Transform your life and your future a little bit at a time by changing what you allow to come into your mind, and what you consciously consent to or pass along as unworthy of your attention. That works equally well for Christian, Jew, Muslim, Hindu, agnostic, or atheist. But once you start on that journey of self-discovery, be prepared for a long one. Once it starts, it never ends...like it or not. As the Buddhist master, Chogyam Trungpa, wrote in his book *Spiritual Materialism,* "About consciousness, it's better never to begin. But once one begins, it's better never to quit."

The fact is, you can't quit once you start because you won't want to. You'll discover things about the mysteries of Life that even from the start will change your life for the better, even if it doesn't appear to be that way at first. People you meet and chance encounters and opportunities will occur that you would not ordinarily even notice. Even when troubling things happen, you will discover certain paradoxes and ironies are really opportunities for growth and continued awakening. You will understand things without having to mentally evaluate or figure them out. You will be better connected to your intuition, which is God-given inner guidance. Call it "Holy Spirit," a "Sixth Sense" or human spirit. It doesn't matter. It will set you on a path to personal freedom that you will never want to abandon.

"With courage, anything is possible," I generally inscribe in books I autograph for people. That's because it's true. So it is with every topic about which I've written in this book, but none quite so definitively nor with such lasting results as being awake and in touch with your own human spirit. On that I can guarantee success to the extent that you believe in it, embrace it, and apply it to your life. For some, it involves some degree of suffering in order to break through to not suffering so much. I don't think one has to suffer, although it does accelerate and amplify the process. By challenging everything you hold dear, which, on an emotional level might feel like suffering, it speeds up and deepens the process. But now you know that you get to choose how to feel about making changes. To the degree you are willing to let go of the suffering and reactionary way of living, and remain awake and observant, you will get to where you most want to go, and to *be*…fully awake, clear and creating your life instead of living in reaction to it.

My heartiest best wishes to each of you, and to those willing to step on board their own seafaring vessel of life, I say

Bon Voyage

…come on in. The water's fine.

Resources

List of Favorite Books, Movies and Other Resources

Because I often refer to certain books, movies and workshop and seminar facilitators and teachers who have inspired me the most, people often ask me for a list of my favorites. In the following pages, I have listed many in each category that were most impactful on me... some that date back a few years, but every one of them worth reading and adding to your own personal library if you have one, or, in the case of movies, watching...even if you have to spring for the few dollars it costs to buy or rent them.

Some of the seminars and workshops I've referenced may no longer be functioning, but many of their lectures and study material are accessible online, and I highly recommend that you do some research. Wisdom has no age limits or shelf life, so don't be deterred if you don't find anything at first. The knowledge is out there for you to seek and find.

First and foremost of all that I can endorse that is truly the best of the many that I attended over the years is Omega-Vector, of Phoenix, Arizona. Their founder, George Addair, has passed over to his "next level of expression," as he would put it with a wry smile. His teachings are still available free of charge, and seminar training has recently resumed at all four levels by accomplished teachers and facilitators trained by George. Omega Vector embraces most of the principles about which I have written, which I had the privilege of learning first-hand from the man himself over several illuminating years. For more information, see https://theomegavector.org., or contact them at info@theomegavector.org.

Another excellent source of unlimited inspiration, fascinating possibilities and shifting points of view and outlook on life changes is the online streaming network, Gaia. There is a virtually limitless selection of documentaries and scientific material that provides exceptionally well-produced and researched information on healthy living and alternative realities. For detailed information, see www.gaia.com

Once you delve into Omega, Gaia or any of the below teachings, films, books or seminars, doors will open for you that will lead you in the right direction. There is no "right" or "wrong" direction. Learning is whatever you do with what lessons you draw to yourself…negative or positive. Some of the most powerful lessons I learned came from the most negative circumstances. Everything is a learning experience, however the more you learn, the less "negative" the lessons you will draw to yourself…or, as the woman in one of the chapters said to me so wryly, "you'll get through them quicker."

Some will feel interesting and exciting, others might not. But any of these will provide you with a place to begin or, if you've been on a spiritual path for a while, it's a way to continue or to accelerate the process. Much of this…even a good many of the movies listed…are based on true stories and actual experiences of people just like you who plunged in (or like me, were pushed or fell in), and had to learn to swim.

You see, we are all "teachers, learners and doers," as Richard Bach wrote in *Illusions; Adventures of a Reluctant Messiah*. Some people are more actively pursuing greater knowledge and awareness, others don't want to know, or care to know. But many people, I believe, are only holding back and waiting for something to be revealed before they dive in. They wait on the edge of the pool, knowing the water's cold, but once they dive in they adjust and are glad they got in.

Either way, any of the following material should be helpful to you as sources of information and inspiration that will help you embrace and understand the process better, and perhaps make the "cold water" more enjoyable and rewarding.

Books

Avalanche; Heretical Views on the Light and the Dark – Wm Brugh Joy, M.D.

Joy's Way – Wm Brugh Joy, M.D.

Man's Search For Meaning – Victor Frankl

Meetings With Remarkable Men (and Women) – G.I. Gurdjieff, 1993

The Great Thoughts – Compiled by George Seldes, 1985

A Universe of Consciousness – Edelman & Tononi, 2000

The Way Things Are – Huston Smith, 2003

Half-Hours with the Best Thinkers – Edited by Frank Finamore, 1999

Spirituality for the Skeptic – Robert Solomon, 2002

21 Lessons for the 21st Century – Yuval Noah Harari, 2019

Illusions; Adventures of a Reluctant Messiah – Richard Bach

Jonathan Livingston Seagull – Richard Bach

The Fifth Sacred Thing – Starhawk

The Journey Home – Lee Carroll

Love: What Life Is All About – Leo Buscaglia

Power vs Force – David Hawkins

Separate Reality - Carlos Casteneda

Spiritual Materialism – Chogyam Trongpa

The Four Agreements – Miguel Ruiz

The Power of Now – Eckhart Tolle

Way of the Peaceful Warrior – Dan Millman

Movies

(Author's Note: These are all favorites, but not just because they're entertaining. Each one portrays or exemplifies the principles about which I have written (courage, passion, integrity, determination, etc. Those marked with an * are exceptionally so, but each and all of them are inspiring and memorable…worth collecting and sharing with others in "movie marathons.")

*A Beautiful Mind – (2001; Russell Crow, Ed Harris, Jennifer Connolly)
Aladdin, Prince of Thieves (1992; Robin Williams)
Always – (1989; Richard Dreyfuss, Holly Hunter, Audrey Hepburn)
*Amadeus (1984; Tom Hulce)
*Antwone Fisher (2002; Denzel Washington)
Bliss (1997; Terrence Stamp)
Chicago – (2002; Catherine Zeta Jones, Richard Gere, Rene Zellweger)
*Copying Beethoven – (2006; Richard Harris, Diane Kruger)
Crash – (2004; Sandra Bullock, Matt Dillon)
Dances With Wolves – (1990; Kevin Costner)
Dangerous Beauty – (1998; Catherine McCormack, Oliver Platt, Jacqueline Bisset)
*Excalibur – (1981; Helen Mirren, Nigel Terry)
*Field of Dreams – (1989; Kevin Costner, Mary McDonnell, Graham Greene)
*First Knight – (1995; Richard Gere, Sean Connery, Julia Ormand)
Flashdance – (Jennifer Beals)
*Ghost – (1990; Patrick Swayze, Demi Moore, Woopie Goldberg)
*Gladiator – (2000; Russell Crowe, Joaquin Phoenix, Richard Harris)
*Good Will Hunting – (1997; Matt Damon, Ben Affleck, Robin Williams)

*Green Mile – (1999; Tom Hanks, David Morse, Michael Clark)
Ground Hog Day – (1993; Bill Murray, Andie McDowell)
*It Could Happen To You – (1994; Nicholas Cage, Bridget Fonda)
*Jerry McGuire – (1996; Tom Cruise, Renee Zellweger, Cuba Gooding Jr.)
*Leap Of Faith – (1992; Steve Martin, Debra Winger)
*Life As A House – (2001; Kevin Kline, Kristin Scott Thomas, Mary Steenburgen)
Mr. Holland's Opus (1995; Richard Dreyfuss, Olympia Dukakis, William H. Macy)
*Murder In The First – (1995; Kevin Bacon, Christian Slater, Gary Oldman)
*Out of Africa – (1985; Robert Redford, Meryl Streep)
Patch Adams – (1998; Robin Williams, Phillip Seymore Hoffman)
*Pay It Forward – (2000; Kevin Spacey, Helen Hunt)
Powder – (1995; Mary Steenburgen, Jeff Goldblum)
Quest For Fire (1981; Ray Dawn Chong, Ron Perlman, Everett McGill)
Radio – (2003; Cuba Gooding, Jr., Ed Harris)
Remember the Titans – (2000; Denzel Washington, Ryan Gosling)
*Rudy – (1993; Sean Astin, Ned Beatty)
*Schindler's List – (1993; Liam Neeson, Ralph Fiennes, Ben Kingsley)
Shawshank Redemption – (1994; Morgan Freeman, Tim Robbins)
Somewhere In Time – (1980; Christopher Reeves, Jane Seymore)
Steel Magnolias – (1989; Sally Field, Julia Roberts, Shirley Maclaine, Olympia Dukakis)
*The Blind Side (2009; Sandra Bullock, Tim McGraw, Kathy Bates)
*The Rookie – (2002; Dennis Quaid)
The Secret – (2006; Jack Canfield, Lisa Nichols, Bob Proctor, Michael Beckwith)

Resources

The Notebook – (2004; Ryan Gosling, Rachel McAdams, James Garner)
*The Verdict – (1982; Paul Newman, Jack Warden)
The Visitor – (2007; Richard Jenkins, Maggie Moore)
*What Dreams May Come – (1998; Robin Williams, Cuba Gooding, Jr., Max von Sydow)
What the Bleep (2004; Marlee Matlin, Joe Dispenza, Fred Alan Wolf)

Workshops

Caroline Myss; https://www.myss.com
Deepok Chopra; https://chopra.com
Esther Hicks ("The Law of Attraction); https://www.abraham-hicks.com
Hay House Publishing; www.hayhouse.com
Leo Buscaglia; www.buscaglia.com
Lee Carroll; www.en.wikipedia.org/wiki/Lee_Carroll
Marianne Williamson; www.marianne.com
Neville Goddard; www.nevillegoddard, www.hubs.com
The Secret; www.thesecret.tv
Wayne Dwyer; www.drwaynedyer.com

For more information about
Beyond The Chaos and other books
by Don Kirchner,
or to sign up for our newsletter, go to
www.amatteroftime.org

About The Author

A former combat helicopter pilot in Vietnam, Don Kirchner spent two and a half years in federal prison for his involvement with a large-scale marijuana smuggling operation in the mid-1980's.

In over 25 years of work in prison and criminal justice reform since his release in 1988, Don has earned commendations from law enforcement and correctional authorities, and numerous government, civic and clerical leaders for his work in assisting inmates and formerly incarcerated individuals in better understanding how to overcome adversity.

Founder and Director of an Arizona nonprofit organization, *Society for Return To Honor*, Don has written two books on turning adversity into personal achievement. He travels extensively in his efforts to assist communities in redirecting juvenile and former adult offenders toward creating better, more meaningful lives and futures.

His recently completed third book, *Jewel Of Saigon*, is a romance novel based upon a memoir, and awaits final editing, review and publication.

Made in the USA
Las Vegas, NV
09 November 2023